Inside the
SECRET GARDEN

A Treasury of Crafts,
Recipes, and Activities

Carolyn Strom Collins
and
Christina Wyss Eriksson

Illustrations by
Tasha Tudor *and* Mary Collier

■ HarperCollins*Publishers*

Dedicated to Lynn and Sheila,
our comrades and friends in pursuit
of *The Secret Garden*
—C.S.C. and C.W.E.

To Phil:
Your love and support keep me moving
forward. You are my one and only.
XOXO
—M.C.

Art on pages i, vi, 4, 5, and 119 by Tasha Tudor.
Photographs are used by permission of Penny Deupree.

Inside the Secret Garden: A Treasury of Crafts, Recipes, and Activities
Text copyright © 2001 by Carolyn Collins and Christina Eriksson
Illustrations copyright © 2001 by Mary Collier
Tasha Tudor illustrations copyright © 1962, renewed 1990 by HarperCollins Publishers

Library of Congress Cataloging-in-Publication Data
Collins, Carolyn Strom.
    Inside the secret garden : a treasury of crafts, recipes, and activities / Carolyn Strom
Collins, Christina Wyss Eriksson ; illustrations by Mary Collier.
        p.   cm.
Summary: A treasury of crafts, activities, recipes, and detailed historical information about
and inspired by Frances Hodgson Burnett's classic novel "The Secret Garden."
    ISBN 0-06-027922-2.
    1. Burnett, Frances Hodgson, 1849–1924. Secret garden—Juvenile literature. 2.
Children's stories, American—History and criticism—Juvenile literature. 3. Gardens in
literature—Juvenile literature. 4. Nature in literature—History and criticism. [1. Burnett,
Frances Hodgson, 1849–1924. Secret garden. 2. American literature—History and
criticism. 3. Gardens in literature.] I. Eriksson, Christina Wyss. II. Tudor, Tasha, ill. III.
Collier, Mary, ill., date. IV. Burnett, Frances Hodgson, 1849–1924. Secret garden. V. Title.
PS1214.S43 C66 2001   99-086350
813'.4—dc21   CIP
                                                                                      AC

Typography by Carla Weise
1 2 3 4 5 6 7 8 9 10
❖
First Edition

Acknowledgments

*W*e are indebted to many helpful people who enthusiastically supported our efforts to uncover the secrets that lay buried in Frances Hodgson Burnett's *The Secret Garden*:

Lynn Mercer and Sheila Page, our tireless, cheerful, knowledgeable, indulgent friends, natives of Yorkshire, volunteered vacation days to chauffeur and direct us through London, York, Castleford, Ferrybridge, New Fryston, Monk Fryston, Airedale, Leeds, Haworth, Whitby, and North Yorkshire Moors National Park. They also gave us all sorts of invaluable information on Yorkshire lore. They pointed out heather, gorse, and broom on the Yorkshire moors and patiently waited by the roadside while we photographed what must have seemed to them the most mundane of subjects. They are also experts on finding the best pubs for the most excellent lunches in Yorkshire.

Frances Hodgson Burnett's great-granddaughter Penny Deupree graciously allowed us to use her photographs of Frances in the biography section, and we were pleased that one result of writing this book was getting to know Penny. Her friend Dot McAlpine made copies of the photographs for our use.

The reference librarians in the libraries of York and Castleford were particularly helpful in finding the dusty and obscure records for Fryston Hall Estate. Eileen Winn Coulson, a resident of Castleford, showed us exactly how to find the original Fryston Hall property.

The administrator for Great Maytham Hall was very generous to let us roam over the estate and study the gardens that had meant so much to Frances when she lived there. The gardeners working in the "Secret Garden" itself were very indulgent of our questions and note taking there. Mrs. P. J. Gartside, resident of Great Maytham Hall, kindly showed us about the interior of the hall, pointing out some of the modernizations as well as some of the historically significant points.

Our hosts at the George Hotel in Cranbrook were very hospitable to us while we were in Kent and helped us understand much about the history and culture in that part of England.

Librarians at the University of Minnesota, the Hennepin and Ramsey County libraries, and the Andersen Horticultural Library found biographical, geographical, sociological, culinary, and horticultural information for us to study. Staff at Kew Gardens, the Chelsea Flower Show, Hampton Court Palace, Harrod's, and Fortnum & Mason were also helpful.

Our editors at HarperCollins, Kara Vicinelli, Tara Weikum, and Alix Reid, were supportive and encouraging in this and many other projects. Our literary agent, Jeanne Hanson, gave us invaluable advice, as always. And we are very grateful to the talented Mary Collier, who so beautifully illustrated this volume.

Finally, we thank most sincerely our husbands, Andy and Mark, for their unfailing encouragement in the research and writing of this book.

—C.S.C.
—C.W.E.

Contents

Introduction

For those who love classics of children's literature, *The Secret Garden* is invariably on the list of favorites. Perhaps it is the garden itself that is so intriguing—walled and mysterious, a wonderful secluded space in which to play and dream undisturbed. Or perhaps it is the mixture of odd characters in the book from "upstairs" and "below stairs." All these elements converge in *The Secret Garden* to make it one of the most enduring and well-known children's books ever written.

After one finishes *The Secret Garden*, questions arise that cannot always be answered, such as "Was the secret garden a real place?" "Was there really a robin like the one who lived in the secret garden?" "What did the secret garden look like?" We wanted to answer some of the questions that arose when we had read it, first as children, and later with our daughters.

To understand any book more fully, it helps to know something about the person who wrote the book, the historical period in which the author set the story, and the geographical location in which the story takes place. We began our work on *Inside the Secret Garden* by reading about Frances Hodgson Burnett.

We were led to several places in England that inspired Burnett's fictional Misselthwaite Manor—most notably Great Maytham Hall in Rolvenden, Kent; the site of Fryston Hall in Yorkshire; and the Yorkshire moors. Visiting these locales helped us envision not only the manor and secret garden itself but also the surrounding landscape.

Both sites have changed considerably since Frances knew them.

Fryston Hall, located on the River Aire south of York, near the towns of Castleford and Ferrybridge, was the home of the Earl of Crewe when Frances came to know it. About ten years after she visited there in 1895, the property was sold. The house stood empty for many years and was finally demolished. The elegant wooded park now sports a gigantic power station where the avenue of lime trees once led the way to the stately home at the top of the hill.

Great Maytham Hall, as it is now known, is located just east of the village of Rolvenden (pronounced "Rolv-dun"). The house was remodeled in 1909 after Frances left it. The well-known architect Sir Edwin Lutyens replaced its Tudor-style facade with the elegant Georgian design seen today. Visitors are permitted to visit the grounds in the summer. The park, the manicured formal gardens, the walled kitchen gardens, and, of course, the walled rose garden that Frances called the secret garden are still maintained, although the trees and roses in the secret garden were replaced years ago. For more information, write to Great Maytham Hall, Rolvenden, Cranbrook, Kent TN17 4NE, Great Britain.

Our goal in writing *Inside the Secret Garden* was to help readers of *The Secret Garden* bring parts of its world into their own. In this book we have included recipes for the foods that Mary and Colin and Dickon ate in the garden, like oatcakes and currant buns. We have listed the kinds of plants and flowers that grew in the secret garden and described how to plant and care for them. We chose some simple games that the children played there and some activities that evoke memories of the secret garden for modern readers.

Now, let's go inside the secret garden and see what we can find.

Chapter One

Frances Hodgson Burnett
and *The Secret Garden*

 Synopsis of *The Secret Garden*

The Secret Garden is Frances Hodgson Burnett's classic nineteenth-century story of how the discovery of a secret garden that had been locked up and neglected for many years changed the life of a little orphan girl.

Mary Lennox was the ten-year-old orphan niece of Archibald Craven, the owner of Misselthwaite Manor, a great estate on the north Yorkshire moors in England. Mary was sent to Misselthwaite Manor from her home in India when her mother and father died in a cholera epidemic.

When Mary first came to the manor, she was sullen and spoiled. Her uncle, still grieving from the death of his wife ten years earlier, provided no comfort other than ordering his staff to see to her needs. Lonely and bored, Mary found it difficult to adjust to her strange, new surroundings. But one of the housemaids, Martha Sowerby, encouraged her to play outside and to explore the extensive gardens of the manor. When Martha mentioned a secret garden, Mary was intrigued and began to wander about the grounds in search of it.

Soon Mary found Ben Weatherstaff, one of the estate's gardeners, digging among the beds in the kitchen garden. A sprightly little robin joined them and seemed to want to make friends with Mary, a new experience for the sour, "nasty-tempered" little girl.

The friendly robin eventually led Mary to find the buried key that opened the the ivy-covered door of the secret garden. As Mary entered the garden, she stared in amazement at the overgrown, tangled vines that covered the trees and shrubbery. She noticed green shoots beginning to thrust through the tough grass and began to dig around them to give them "room to breathe."

The secret garden immediately began to work its magic on Mary, for as she dug in the earth and tried to help the garden come back to life, she herself began to grow and come to life as well. She learned to laugh and to care about something other than herself.

In the process of restoring the secret garden, Mary became friends with Dickon, Martha's younger brother, who had a gift for taming wild birds and animals. He helped her in the garden, bringing along some of his pets—Captain, the fox cub; Soot, the crow; and two squirrels, Nut and Shell.

But there was a mystery inside the manor. Mary heard strange crying noises in the night. Martha and the other servants insisted that it was the wind "wuthering" about the windows, but Mary was not convinced and sought the source of the strange noises. She discovered a boy, about her age, in one of the rooms in the manor. His name was Colin.

Colin was the son of Archibald Craven. He believed he was sick and spent all his time in bed. His bad temper was a trial to the staff, who were under orders to keep Colin's existence a secret. Once Mary found him, however, things began to change.

Mary wheeled Colin about in the sunshine and eventually allowed him to enter the secret garden. Colin, too, was captivated by the magic of the garden and gained strength from working there alongside Mary and Dickon.

As the secret garden began to bloom with daffodils and crocuses, the children bloomed too. By the time the thousands of roses appeared, Mary and Colin discovered their spirits had been restored.

Archibald Craven returned to Misselthwaite Manor after a long trip and found the children in the secret garden. He was shocked to see Colin, the sickly son he had left behind, running around the garden with Mary and Dickon.

The magic of the garden began to work on Mr. Craven, too, as he finally set aside his grief for his wife. The changes, growth, and renewal that had brought the long-neglected secret garden back to life had also changed the lives of Mary and her friends.

Frances Hodgson Burnett at age 22.

Frances Hodgson Burnett

*F*rances Hodgson Burnett was the author of *The Secret Garden*, *A Little Princess*, *Little Lord Fauntleroy*, and many other favorite children's books. She was born in Manchester, England, in 1849, and had two brothers and two sisters. Her father, a prosperous merchant, died when Frances was just four years old.

The family moved from their home on Cheetham Hill Road to live with relatives in Seedley Grove, a village a few miles west of Manchester, then to a house on Islington Square in Salford, a town closer to Manchester. Although she was very young, Frances held many impressions of houses and gardens and people in her memory, which she used much later in her stories.

There were several gardens near the homes where Frances grew up that one day would provide part of the inspiration for *The Secret Garden*. The first was the garden behind Seedley Grove, a place Frances called the "Back Garden of Eden."

It was also at Seedley Grove that Frances made the acquaintance of Emma Rimmer, a little girl who lived nearby. Frances and Emma were about the same age but were from very different backgrounds. Emma spoke with a strong Lancashire accent, and Frances, fascinated by the wonderfully expressive words and phrases, quickly learned it from her. Frances grew up in a middle-class, urban home and had developed a more refined way of speaking than Emma, who had grown up in the country. This was the beginning of Frances's keen interest in dialects, which she made use of in many of her books and stories, including *The Secret Garden*.

Later, when the Hodgson family moved into their house on Islington Square, another garden caught Frances's interest. It was a

Frances with her two sons: Vivian (left), age 12, and Lionel (right), age 14, in 1888

neglected garden behind an abandoned home called Page's Hall, and it was surrounded by a high brick wall. In her autobiography, *The One I Knew Best of All*, Frances described how, one day, the little green door in the wall was open and she "passed through the enchanted door and stood within the mysterious precincts looking around her."

In 1865, Frances and her family sailed to America, settling in Tennessee, where they could be near her uncle and his family. Frances loved Tennessee, although the family struggled to make ends meet. Frances found ways to add to the family income by selling eggs and wild grapes, teaching music, and setting up a "select seminary," or small private school, in their home.

She also began writing. She published her first story, "Hearts and Diamonds" in 1868. She was nineteen years old.

On September 19, 1873, Frances married Dr. Swan Burnett. The couple had two sons, Lionel and Vivian. The family traveled a great deal and lived many places, including Tennessee, Paris, Long Island, London, and Washington, D.C.

Frances continued to write stories for many of the popular magazines of the day—*Godey's Lady's Book, Harper's, Scribner's,* and others. Frances's first book, *That Lass o' Lowrie's,* was published in 1877 in both the United States and England.

In 1885, the children's magazine *St. Nicholas* published, in serial form, what would be one of Frances's most popular novels, *Little*

Lord Fauntleroy. It was published the next year in book form. Later, the story was produced as both a stage play and a film, starring Mary Pickford. Two years later another of Frances's most popular books, *Sara Crewe; or, What Happened at Miss Minchin's* (later rewritten and reissued as *A Little Princess*), was published. Frances had finished it just before sailing to London for Queen Victoria's Golden Jubilee festivities.

While in London, she was introduced to Stephen Townesend, an actor and aspiring playwright. Their friendship grew, and Frances hired him as her business manager.

Most of the 1890s were unhappy years for Frances. Her older son, Lionel, died from consumption, now called tuberculosis. Frances's marriage was crumbling. To distract herself, she did charity work, traveled a great deal, and continued to write.

In December of 1895, Frances received an invitation to a house party at the home of the Earl of Crewe. The sixteen-hundred-acre Yorkshire estate, Fryston Hall, was south of the city of York, in the parish of Ferry Fryston, near Castleford. Frances later described the house in a letter to her son Vivian as "a big, substantial, lovable house in the midst of a park." Though not located in the part of Yorkshire where the moors are, Fryston Hall would later provide Frances with her model for Misselthwaite Manor in *The Secret Garden*.

Frances was very moved by the earl's family circumstances. The earl's young wife, Sybil, had died seven years after their marriage, leaving him with their three daughters. Frances wrote to a friend that the couple had been "radiantly happy and inseparable," and Frances believed that "his eyes are always looking for her and thinking of her." She also observed that "a picture of a pretty, slender girl in a white frock" hung in the Fryston Hall drawing room. It was a portrait of Sybil, painted just before she died.

Frances's memories of the earl who lived at Fryston Hall furnished the basis of Archibald Craven's story in *The Secret Garden*. She even placed a portrait of Colin's mother, who had died when he was born, in Colin's room at Misselthwaite Manor, reminiscent of the one of Sybil in Fryston Hall.

Maytham Hall around 1898

In 1898, Frances and Swan Burnett divorced, and she leased a large estate in the village of Rolvenden, Kent, south of London. It was called Maytham Hall, and it would be her home for the next nine years. She was particularly fond of the old walled garden at Maytham and worked in it often. It became the primary inspiration for *The Secret Garden.*

The gardens of Maytham had been installed when the main house was built in the eighteenth century. There were walled kitchen gardens as well as a walled orchard. When Frances moved into Maytham, the walled orchard was quite overgrown and neglected. Frances was enchanted by the secluded garden and began to clear the weeds away from the trees. She added grass seed and climbing roses, creating a "bower of incredible beauty and fragrance," as her son described it.

Frances's own experience with a robin in her walled garden at Maytham Hall provided the inspiration for the robin in *The Secret Garden.* She wrote a little book about him called *My Robin* in 1912,

SCOTLAND

Yorkshire
Moors
(location of the fictional
MISSELTHWAITE MANOR)

*Irish
Sea*

◆FRYSTON HALL

Manchester

Seedley Grove ◆   ◆ ◆

Salford

ENGLAND

WALES

Bristol Channel

◆London

◆GREAT MAYTHAM HALL

English Channel

after a reader of *The Secret Garden* asked her, "Did you own the original of the robin?"

Frances explained in *My Robin* that, indeed, there was a robin in her rose garden in Kent and that "the surprise was not that he was there but that he *stayed* there." He hopped close to her worktable under one of the trees, he followed her as she strolled about the garden, and he even perched on the wide brim of her hat one day.

Two years after Frances moved into Maytham Hall, she married her business manager, Stephen Townesend. The marriage failed, however, and they separated in 1902. Frances lived at Maytham Hall another five years. Then she left England for the United States in early spring of 1907, planning to settle there. After a year of looking for a suitable site, she bought land on Long Island, overlooking Manhasset Bay, and began building a large home, which she named Plandome Park. She also supervised the installation of another magnificent garden, to remind her of the one at Maytham Hall.

While her house and garden were under construction, Frances began writing *The Secret Garden*, starting it in the spring of 1909 and finishing it about a year later. *The Secret Garden* was published in 1911.

Frances died on October 29, 1924, at the age of seventy-four. She had written over fifty books, as well as numerous plays, short stories, and poems, but she is best remembered for her novel of renewal and redemption, *The Secret Garden*.

Inside the Secret Garden Time Line

When Frances Hodgson Burnett was born in Manchester, England, Queen Victoria had been on the throne for twelve years and was thirty years old. There were twenty-nine states in the United States of America, and the famous California gold rush had begun a year earlier, in 1848. On both sides of the Atlantic, women were fighting for the right to vote.

It was a golden age for the arts. William Wordsworth was poet laureate of England; Charles Dickens was publishing some of his best-known works; Charlotte Brontë's *Jane Eyre* and her sister Emily's *Wuthering Heights* had just been published two years before.

The Industrial Revolution had been under way for decades. Railroads and steamships were revolutionizing transportation and making the world a smaller place.

Wars and other forms of political unrest were taking place all over the world. Europe, Asia, Africa, and the United States were involved in their own conflicts; Great Britain was forming its huge empire by colonizing other countries, including India, known as its "jewel in the crown."

It was a time of great creativity, innovation, and dramatic change, and Frances Hodgson Burnett became a part of it as an author of dozens of books, stories, and poems.

1840s

Edwin Hodgson and Eliza Boond are married; their first three children are born in Manchester, England: Edwin, John George, and Frances Eliza on November 24, 1849

1849

- ◆ *Charles Dickens's* David Copperfield *is published*
- ◆ *Edgar Allan Poe, American author of "The Raven" and "The Pit and the Pendulum," dies*

1850s

Frances's sisters Edith Mary and Edwina are born; Frances's father, Edwin Hodgson, dies; the family moves to Seedley Grove, then back into Manchester; Frances attends the Hadfields' "Select Seminary for Young Ladies and Gentlemen"

1850

- ◆ *Nathaniel Hawthorne's* Scarlet Letter *is published*
- ◆ *California becomes the thirty-first state of the United States*

1851

- ◆ *The horse-drawn double-decker bus is introduced*
- ◆ The New York Times *begins publication*

1852

- ◆ *Harriet Beecher Stowe's* Uncle Tom's Cabin *is published*

1855

- ◆ *Charlotte Brontë, author of* Jane Eyre, *dies*
- ◆ *Walt Whitman's* Leaves of Grass *is published*

1857

◆ *Sepoy Rebellion in India; the rule of the British East India Company is terminated and a viceroy (representative of the British crown) is appointed*

1859

◆ *Charles Dickens's* Tale of Two Cities *and Alfred Lord Tennyson's* Idylls of the King *are published*

◆ *Construction on the Suez Canal, planned to link the Mediterranean and Red Seas, begins*

1860s

The Hodgson family leaves England and settles in New Market, Tennessee; Frances's first published work appears in *Godey's Lady's Book*; a second story, "Miss Carruthers' Engagement," is published a few months later

1860

◆ Godey's Lady's Book *begins publication*

◆ *Abraham Lincoln is elected president of the United States*

1861

◆ *Civil War begins in the United States*

◆ *Prince Albert, Queen Victoria's husband, dies*

◆ *Queen Victoria institutes the Order of the Star of India*

1863

◆ *Construction begins on London's underground system*

1865

◆ *Lewis Carroll's* Alice in Wonderland *is published*

◆ *Abraham Lincoln is assassinated in Washington; Andrew Johnson becomes president*

◆ *The Civil War ends in the United States*

1867

◆ *The Dominion of Canada is established*

◆ *The United States buys Alaska from Russia*

1868

◆ *Louisa May Alcott's* Little Women *is published*

1869

◆ *The Suez Canal is completed, reducing the time needed for the voyage from India to England from four months to about seventeen days*

1870s

Frances's mother, Eliza Hodgson, dies; Frances goes to New York; she meets Richard Watson Gilder of *Scribner's Monthly* magazine; Frances returns to Tennessee and marries Swan Burnett on September 19, 1873; Lionel Burnett is born; the Burnetts move to Paris so Swan can study medicine; Vivian is born in Paris; Frances's *That Lass o' Lowrie's* appears in installment form in *Scribner's Monthly*; Frances publishes nine more books in the next two years

1870

◆ *Charles Dickens, British author of* A Christmas Carol *and many other novels, dies*

1871

◆ *Louisa May Alcott's* Little Men *and George Eliot's* Middlemarch *are published*

1873

◆ *Famine in Bengal, India*

1875

◆ *Hans Christian Andersen, Danish author of fairy tales, dies*
◆ *Mary Baker Eddy publishes* Science and Health, *explaining her Christian Science philosophy*

1876

◆ *Mark Twain's* Tom Sawyer *is published*
◆ *Queen Victoria is proclaimed empress of India*

1877

◆ *Anna Sewell's* Black Beauty *is published*
◆ *Thomas Edison invents the phonograph*

1880s

Frances visits Emily Dickinson's home in Amherst, Massachusetts; Oscar Wilde visits Frances at her home in Washington, D.C.; Frances's *Little Lord Fauntleroy* begins in serial form in *St. Nicholas*; *Little Lord Fauntleroy* is published in book form and becomes a best-seller; Frances takes Lionel and Vivian to London for Queen Victoria's Golden Jubilee celebration; she becomes friends with author Henry James and meets Stephen Townesend for the first time; Frances's *Sara Crewe* is published and is a great success

1883
◆ *Robert Louis Stevenson's* Treasure Island *is published*

1884
◆ *Mark Twain's* Huckleberry Finn *is published*
◆ The Oxford English Dictionary *begins publication*

1885
◆ *The Indian National Congress is founded*

1887
◆ *Queen Victoria's Golden Jubilee celebrates her 50th year on the throne*
◆ *Arthur Conan Doyle publishes "A Study in Scarlet," the first of the Sherlock Holmes stories*

1888
◆ *Louisa May Alcott dies*

1889
◆ *The Eiffel Tower is completed in Paris*
◆ *North and South Dakota, Montana, and Washington become states*

1890s

Frances's older son, Lionel, dies of tuberculosis in France; Frances writes *The One I Knew Best of All*, the story of her childhood; Frances visits Fryston Hall, estate of the Earl of Crewe, in Yorkshire; Frances and Swan Burnett divorce; Frances rents Maytham Hall near Rolvenden, Kent, in England

1890
◆ *Moving pictures debut*

1893
◆ Vogue *magazine is launched*

1894
◆ *Rudyard Kipling's* Jungle Book *is published*

1897
◆ *Amelia Earhart, first woman to fly solo across the Atlantic Ocean, is born*

1900s

Frances marries her business manager, Stephen Townesend, but they separate in 1902; Frances becomes an American citizen; Swan Burnett, Frances's first husband, dies; Frances returns to the United States, where she purchases her estate, Plandome Park, on Long Island; she begins work on *The Secret Garden*

1901
◆ *Queen Victoria dies at age eighty-two; her son, Edward VII, ascends to the throne*

1902
◆ *Beatrix Potter's* Tale of Peter Rabbit *is published*

1903
◆ *Kate Douglas Wiggin's* Rebecca of Sunnybrook Farm *is published*

1904
◆ *James Barrie's* Peter Pan *is published*

1908
◆ *L. M. Montgomery's* Anne of Green Gables *and Kenneth Grahame's* Wind in the Willows *are published*

1909
◆ *Admiral Perry reaches the North Pole*

1910s

The Secret Garden and *My Robin* are published; Frances's son Vivian marries Constance Buel; Frances's granddaughters, Verity and Dorin, are born; Stephen Townesend, Frances's second husband, dies

1910
◆ *Halley's comet appears*
◆ *Sir Edwin Lutyens, famed British architect, redesigns Maytham Hall; it is remodeled in Georgian style, which it has retained to the present day*

1912
◆ *The* Titanic *sinks*
◆ *Delhi becomes the capital of India (moved from Calcutta)*
◆ *New Mexico and Arizona become the 47th and 48th states of the United States*

1913

◆ *Eleanor Porter's* Pollyanna *is published*

1914

◆ *World War I begins*
◆ *The Panama Canal opens*

1917

◆ *United States enters World War I*
◆ *Mary Pickford stars in the film adaption of*
   A Little Princess

1918

◆ *World War I ends*
◆ *Influenza epidemic begins*
◆ *Johnny Gruelle's* Raggedy Ann Stories *is published*

1919

◆ *The League of Nations is established*

1920s

Frances Hodgson Burnett dies at her home, Plandome Park, on October 29, 1924, at the age of 74

1920

◆ *U.S. Congress passes the Nineteenth Amendment of the Constitution, giving women the vote*

1922

◆ *Emily Post's* Etiquette *is published*
◆ *The tomb of Egyptian pharoah Tutankhamen is discovered*

1923

◆ *Stanley Baldwin is elected prime minister of Great Britain*

1924

◆ *Calvin Coolidge is elected president of the United States*
◆ *E. M. Forster's* A Passage to India *is published*

Chapter Two

Misselthwaite Manor
and Gardens

 ## The Manor House and Grounds

"The house is six hundred years old and it's on the edge of the moor, and there's near a hundred rooms in it, though most of them's shut up and locked. And there's pictures and fine old furniture and things that's been there for ages, and there's a big park round it and gardens and trees with branches trailing to the ground."

Misselthwaite Manor, the home of the Craven family in *The Secret Garden*, was a fictional estate set in the northern moors of Yorkshire. The centerpiece of the estate was the large, low stone house. It was surrounded by hundreds of acres of wooded lands called a park, fields and pastures, kitchen gardens, and flower gardens. Cottages that housed the manor staff were scattered about the estate.

The Secret Garden is set on the Yorkshire moors, windswept, seemingly barren hills. They are sparsely settled, even today.

When Mary first encountered the moors on the way to Misselthwaite Manor, she asked Mrs. Medlock, "It's—it's not the sea, is it?" "No, not it," answered Mrs. Medlock. "Nor it isn't fields nor mountains, it's just miles and miles and miles of wild land that nothing grows on but heather and gorse and broom, and nothing lives on but wild ponies and sheep."

However, when Mary asked the housemaid Martha about the moorland, Martha talked about it in glowing terms: "I just love it. It's none bare. It's covered wi' growing things as smells sweet. It's fair lovely in spring an' summer when th' gorse an' broom an' heather's in flower. . . . Eh! I wouldn't live away from th' moor for anythin'." Martha and her younger brother Dickon had grown up on the moors, learning to appreciate the fresh, clean air and the purple heather that grows all over them.

While Mary, Colin, and Dickon spent most of their time at Misselthwaite in the secret garden, they also played in the park, a large wooded area that is a common feature of manors and country estates in England. Mary wandered along the paths in the park when she first began exploring Misselthwaite, and she met Dickon there for the first time. A memorable scene in *The Secret Garden* depicts

the children roasting eggs and potatoes in a little stone oven they made in the park.

As at most manor houses, the focus of the Misselthwaite house was the great hall, a large room where visitors were received. In a typical manor house, the hall was impressively decorated, usually with the family's collections of artworks, suits of armor, ancient weaponry, flags, and tapestries. In *The Secret Garden* the hall of Misselthwaite Manor was furnished with suits of armor and plenty of landscapes and portraits.

There were more pictures in another large long room called the gallery. This gallery of paintings at Misselthwaite Manor was typical of large country houses. Portraits of ancestors were painted by the best artists of the day, and elaborate frames were constructed especially for the portraits. The gallery itself provided a place for walks and contemplation; Mary and Colin used Misselthwaite's portrait gallery for exercise when bad weather kept them inside.

Surrounding the hall on the ground floor were other formal rooms—drawing rooms, dining rooms, a library, a smoking room, several parlors, and various service rooms. A grand staircase and several lesser staircases, mostly for servants to use, led to other floors where bedroom suites, a nursery, and various storage rooms were located. Many of the rooms at Misselthwaite Manor were locked up, but Archibald Craven, his son, Colin, and Mary all had their own bedroom suites.

On the ground floor and in the basement of a typical manor house were the kitchen, servants' hall, scullery, and private rooms for some of the servants such as the butler, housekeeper, and house steward. There were many rooms for special uses. The butler's pantry contained dishes and serving pieces for the table; "strong rooms" secured valuables; a lamp room provided storage for kerosene lamps as well as a place to clean the lamps and refill them; and wine and

beer cellars and several pantries kept vast supplies of beverages and foods.

Like any large manor, Misselthwaite would have had many outbuildings, each devoted to a special task. A laundry or washhouse contained several large rooms for cleaning all the clothes and linens used at the manor. The washing room was furnished with troughs for washing and rinsing. More large rooms were designated for drying, mangling, and ironing. (A mangle was an ironing contraption with wide heated rollers through which tablecloths and sheets could be pressed.) There was also an enclosed yard for drying clothes in the sunshine.

Nearby were a bakehouse, bottle store (wine cellar), gun rooms, painter's shop, and coal houses. A large bungalow housed the staff who worked in these buildings. Stables were a short distance from the mansion, screened by a stand of trees and a high stone wall. The stablehands were housed in rooms over the stables. Farther back from the mansion were more farm buildings. A cowshed, piggeries, henhouses, cart shed, carpenter's shop, blacksmith's shop, and cottages for the workers were grouped together.

Houses and cottages scattered all over the estate housed the bailiff, gardeners, gatekeepers, gamekeeper, and field workers. Hunting lodges were available for use when the owner and his guests wanted to shoot game in the large wooded areas on the estate.

An estate like Misselthwaite Manor was large enough to produce almost everything the residents needed, and served as home, workplace, and community.

The Staff

In this queer place one scarcely ever saw any one at all. In fact, there was no one to see but the servants, and when their master was away they lived a luxurious life below stairs, where there was a huge kitchen hung about with shining brass and pewter, and a large servants' hall where there were four or five abundant meals eaten every day, and where a great deal of lively romping went on when Mrs. Medlock was out of the way.

There was a rigid hierarchy in the "downstairs" society, as the household servants were sometimes called. The housekeeper, butler, cook, house steward, valet, and lady's maid were considered "upper servants"; housemaids, kitchen and scullery maids, and others were known as "lower servants." Many were descended from families that had lived and worked on the same estate for generations.

In *The Secret Garden*, we are introduced to a few of the staff who worked at Misselthwaite Manor.

Mrs. Medlock, the housekeeper, was in charge of all the female servants at Misselthwaite Manor. She made sure their duties were performed correctly, training them when necessary. The symbol of her post was a large ring of keys that opened pantries and storerooms, linen closets, and other rooms in the manor in her charge.

Martha, the housemaid who befriended Mary, was required to rise very early in the morning so that she could light the kitchen fire, clean the fireplaces in the parlors and dining room, dust and sweep the main rooms, light fires in the bedrooms, and bring in hot water for baths. All these duties were performed before she was allowed to eat her breakfast! She also made the beds, mended linen, helped set the table for family meals, prepared tea, answered the door, and attended to many other chores ordered by Mrs. Medlock.

Mrs. Loomis, the cook, was in charge of planning all the meals at the manor. She consulted with the head gardener on which vegetables and herbs to plant in the kitchen gardens, kept the kitchen pantries stocked, ordered ingredients that were needed, put up jams and jellies in season, and supervised the cooking of breakfast, luncheon, tea, and dinner.

A nurse was on the staff at Misselthwaite Manor since Colin was, or thought himself to be, an invalid. She lived in rooms near Colin's suite in order to be on hand at all times to feed, bathe, and entertain him, and to administer his medications and tonics.

The butler's duties included supervising the male servants in the house. He checked the dining table before meals were served to be sure everything was in order and also helped serve. He kept the silver serving pieces polished perfectly, made sure the house was locked up at night, and announced visitors.

There were several footmen at Misselthwaite Manor. They delivered messages for Mr. Craven, rode on the back of the carriage to watch for dangers along the road, and made sure the occupants of the carriage were comfortable during journeys. John, the strongest footman, carried Colin back and forth to his room when he began to go outside with Mary and Dickon. One of the footmen at Misselthwaite accompanied the carriage from the railway station when Mary and Mrs. Medlock rode to the manor the first time. The footmen also attended to duties around the main house, such as cleaning lamps, carrying wood and coal, and helping set the table and serve the meals.

Mr. Pitcher was Archibald Craven's valet and one of the few people Mr. Craven saw. According to Mrs. Medlock, Mr. Pitcher "took care of him when he was a child and he knows his ways." As valet, Mr. Pitcher was in charge of Mr. Craven's clothing, accompanied him on trips, and took care of any personal errands Mr. Craven required.

Mr. Roach, the head gardener at Misselthwaite, oversaw Ben Weatherstaff and the other undergardeners. He decided what to plant in the gardens and ordered the seeds and other supplies. He oversaw the planting, cultivation, harvesting, and storage of produce and the care of tools.

There were many other servants and workers at Misselthwaite Manor. Kitchen maids helped the cook, and scullery maids cleaned the dishes and pots and pans. Several housemaids, like Martha, kept all the rooms of the house clean and polished. A coachman drove the carriages, and stable hands and grooms cared for the horses. There were countless tasks to be done in such a vast home, and it was necessary to employ a large staff of servants in order for everything to run smoothly.

The Gardens at Misselthwaite Manor

When she had passed through the shrubbery gate she found herself in great gardens, with wide lawns and winding walks with clipped borders.

When Mary began her exploration of the gardens at Misselthwaite, she came first to the formal gardens that surrounded the mansion. There she discovered "trees, and flowerbeds, and evergreens clipped into strange shapes, and a large pool with an old gray fountain in its midst." Wide gravel paths wound through the gardens. These ornamental gardens were typical of a large estate and were designed and maintained especially for the master of the house, his family, and visitors.

Delightful as these gardens were, however, it was the kitchen gardens, orchards, and fields that produced the food to sustain the family, servants, and guests of the manor. An acre of land and two gardeners per acre usually were needed for every twelve people living on a large estate.

There were at least three kitchen gardens at Misselthwaite and an orchard of fruit trees. Each garden was surrounded by high brick walls. The walls kept animals and thieves out and heat in. Heat from the sun warmed the walls during the day, and the bricks held much of that heat through the night. This encouraged the fruit to grow faster and prevented frost damage. Some of the walls had hot-water pipes built into them to further protect the fruits from extreme cold when necessary.

When Mary first wandered into the kitchen gardens, some of them were planted with winter vegetables like turnips, beets, potatoes, onions, and cabbages. Also in the gardens were beds covered by glass that contained more tender plants, such as lettuces, spinach, tomatoes, melons, strawberries, asparagus, herbs, and flower seedlings. The glass covers helped capture the heat of the sun and kept the plants from freezing.

The typical walled orchard contained a variety of fruit trees. Apple, pear, plum, and cherry trees were relatively hardy and could be planted in the open part of the orchard. More delicate fruits, such as peaches and apricots, were planted closer to the walls for support and warmth. Gooseberries, grapes, figs, and currants were planted in the orchard, too.

Mary noticed that some of the fruit trees were trained to grow right on the walls. This technique was developed by the French and

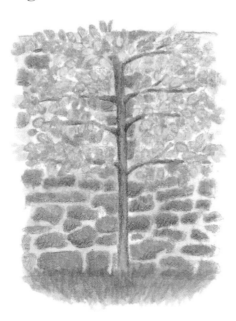

is called *espalier* (pronounced es-PAHL-yay). Espaliered fruit trees produce more fruit because more light and warmth can reach the fruit than if it were growing under a natural shady canopy of leaves.

Storage rooms, toolsheds, potting sheds, and gardeners' quarters were also part of a manor's kitchen garden scheme. It was important to have some of the gardening staff living nearby the gardens so they could cover the plants or keep the water in the pipes heated in cold weather.

The Cottage Garden

The Secret Garden was not the only one Dickon worked in. Round the cottage on the moor there was a piece of ground enclosed by a low wall of rough stones.

Even the humblest cottage on a large estate was likely to have its own kitchen garden. In *The Secret Garden* the Sowerby cottage had one, tended expertly by Dickon. He had planted "potatoes and cabbages, turnips and carrots and herbs" for the family of fourteen who lived in the cottage. The sturdy vegetables grew easily in the cold Yorkshire climate and could be stored for the winter, too. Herbs such as parsley, thyme, dill, and sage were grown for seasoning various dishes as well as for concocting homemade remedies.

But Dickon did not plant just practical vegetables and herbs. He also planted "mignonette and pinks and pansies" and other "bright sweet-scented things" and "tucked moorland foxglove into every crevice" of the low stone wall surrounding the cottage garden.

The average cottage dweller would not be able to afford an expensive brick wall to enclose his garden like the ones at the manor. Instead, he would have built a wall of stones collected from the nearby countryside to keep winds and large animals out of the garden. For even more protection, he might have dug some of the soil out of the garden to lower it a foot or two. The Sowerby cottage had this kind of stone-walled garden.

The Secret Garden

"One of th' gardens is locked up. No one has been in it for ten years."

Frances Hodgson Burnett's own secret garden at Maytham Hall and the friendly robin who kept her company when she worked there inspired *The Secret Garden*.

When Mary finally found the door to the garden, she discovered the garden was quite large, about half an acre, completely surrounded by thick brick walls ten feet high. Stone benches were placed strategically around the garden. An old sundial, overgrown with rose branches, was one of the few ornaments. Large trees grew in the secret garden, and fruit trees had been espaliered against the brick walls. Wide paths were laid out in a geometric pattern, outlining the flower beds.

The garden was overgrown and quite wild, having been neglected for ten years. The wide paths were cluttered with grass and weeds; the urns were covered in moss, and the plants in them were dead. The espaliered fruit trees needed expert pruning to bring them back to their intended shapes. The rose stems had grown all over the trees and were tangled in thorny masses everywhere. Still, the garden was a wondrous sight to Mary when she first stepped into it.

The high walls had helped protect the fruit trees and roses

that Mr. and Mrs. Craven had
planted there years earlier. Ben
Weatherstaff later admitted
that he had come into the
garden each year to care for
the roses as he had once prom-
ised Mrs. Craven he would do.
But the garden had largely been
left alone and seemed to be
waiting for Mary and Colin and
Dickon to revive it.

The first signs showing Mary
there was still life in the secret
garden were little green shoots
beginning to thrust through the
thick grass. These turned out to
be crocuses, daffodils, narcissuses, snowdrops, iris, and other spring
bulbs, along with lilies of the valley. The secret garden was carpeted
with them.

Soon other flowers began to bud—columbine, delphiniums, and
lilies. Dickon brought packets of poppy, blue larkspur, and
mignonette seeds for sowing in the garden.

The roses, of course, were the centerpiece of the garden. There
were many different kinds of roses there. Standard roses are tall, like
small trees. Climbing roses sent out long stems and were planted
next to tree trunks, fences, walls, trellises, and arbors so that they
would have something to climb up and over. Smaller shrub roses
were planted in beds or borders.

Mary and Dickon and Colin worked every day in the secret garden,
pulling weeds, watering, and planting. But they didn't want to make
it a "gardener's garden, all clipped an' spick an' span" like the formal
ornamental gardens surrounding Misselthwaite. They kept it as they
thought a secret garden should be, "with things runnin' wild, an'
swingin' an' catchin' hold of each other."

Chapter Three

Secret Garden Breakfasts and Teas: Menus and Recipes

The morning that Dickon . . . went behind a big rosebush and brought forth two tin pails and revealed that one was full of rich new milk with cream on the top of it, and that the other held cottage-made currant buns folded in a clean blue and white napkin, buns so carefully tucked in that they were still hot, there was a riot of surprised joyfulness.

Neither Colin nor Mary had much appetite in the beginning of *The Secret Garden*. But their work to restore the garden brought about many changes in both of them. The time they spent in the fresh air and sunshine, along with the exercise they got while weeding and pruning and planting, increased their interest in the bountiful breakfasts and the hearty evening meals prepared for them.

At first Mary and Colin tried to keep their newly robust appetites and their work in the garden a secret. It was not easy for them, though. The cook at the manor provided all sorts of delicious dishes, and Mrs. Sowerby, Martha and Dickon's mother, frequently sent the children freshly baked bread and rolls from her cottage kitchen. Dickon often arrived at the garden with a pail of creamy fresh milk and oatcakes or buns for the three to share at noontime.

Afternoon tea is an institution all over the British Isles and is served between lunch and dinner, usually about four o'clock. It can be quite an elegant occasion with several courses, a silver tea service, and fine china. Usually, however, it is a small meal with sandwiches and cakes and, of course, tea, or an evening meal known as "high tea" with more substantial fare. These days it is often simply tea and toast or just tea alone as a break in the afternoon's activity.

If you would like to serve your own secret garden breakfasts and teas, here are some menus and recipes that will help you re-create many of the ones that Mary, Colin, and Dickon enjoyed as they brought their garden back to life.

Important cooking tips:

Any time you are using sharp objects, or electrical or heating appliances, an adult must be present.

It is recommended that you have some basic kitchen essentials on hand. These include:

- Pots and pans, including small and large nonstick skillets, cookie sheets, muffin tins, and bread loaf pans
- Utensils such as knives, forks, spoons, spatulas, and wooden spoons
- Small, medium, and large mixing bowls and colanders
- Baking tools such as pastry blenders, rolling pins, cutting boards and bread boards, wire racks
- Appliances like electric mixers and eggbeaters
- Miscellaneous supplies like towels and plastic wrap

Also, it is important to read every recipe before starting to cook to be sure you have all the necessary ingredients.

A POT OF TEA

Since the eighteenth century, a pot of tea has traditionally accompanied meals served throughout Great Britain and will be a part of each secret garden tea, too. Here is how to make a proper pot of tea.

You will need:

6 cups cold water
1 cup hot water
6 teaspoons loose tea (English breakfast, Darjeeling, and Earl Grey are popular varieties in Yorkshire and the rest of England) or 2–3 teabags

A tea strainer
OPTIONAL:
Sugar, milk, lemon slices

1. Fill a kettle with the cold water. Set it on high heat and bring the water to a boil.

2. While the kettle is heating, put hot water in a teapot to warm it. Set the teapot aside.

3. Just before the water in the kettle begins to boil, pour the water out of the teapot.

4. Spoon the loose tea into the teapot, or hang the teabags inside, if you prefer.

5. Pour the boiling water over the tea leaves and stir them. Put the lid on the teapot and let the tea rest for a few minutes so the flavor will develop fully.

6. When you are ready to serve the tea, pour it into china cups. (If you used loose tea leaves, pour the tea through a tea strainer to keep the leaves out of the cups.) You may add sugar, and milk or a lemon slice, to each cup if you like. If the tea is too strong, add a little hot water to each cup.

Makes 6 cups of tea

Mary's First Breakfast

A table in the center was set with a good substantial breakfast. But she had always had a very small appetite, and she looked with something more than indifference at the first plate Martha set before her.

Mary was not enthusiastic about the traditional Yorkshire breakfast that Martha brought to her on her first morning at Misselthwaite Manor. Mary was used to a typical Indian breakfast—exotic tropical fruits, rice, bread. However, once Mary learned to enjoy the crisp, cool air of the Yorkshire mornings, she "took up her spoon and began to eat" her porridge until the bowl was empty.

If you would like to prepare a typical Yorkshire breakfast like Mary's, start with porridge, toast and marmalade, and, of course, a pot of hot tea.

Porridge

Treacle

Toast and Marmalade

Tea

PORRIDGE

"Tha' doesn't want any porridge!" Martha exclaimed incredulously. . . . "Tha' doesn't know how good it is. Put a bit o' treacle on it or a bit o' sugar."

Porridge can be any kind of cooked cereal—cream of wheat, cream of rice, grits, oats, or other grains cooked in water or milk until they are thick and creamy.

Today we have several varieties of oatmeal to choose from when making porridge, from the ground oatmeal found in England to steel-cut Irish oats to the rolled oats that come in old-fashioned and quick-cooking types and even instant varieties. Mary's Yorkshire version of porridge would have been made from finely ground oatmeal.

While we usually pour milk or cream over our bowl of porridge, Mary probably learned to follow the Yorkshire custom of dipping each spoonful of porridge into a small dish of cream, something you might like to try, too.

To cook this classic porridge, you will need:

⅔ cup water or milk
⅓ cup oatmeal
¼ teaspoon salt
½ cup milk or cream

OPTIONAL:
1 teaspoon butter; 1 or 2 teaspoons treacle (see page 39), white sugar, brown sugar, honey, molasses, or maple syrup; 2 tablespoons raisins, dried cranberries, chopped dates, or other dried fruits

1. Bring the water or milk just to a boil in a heavy-bottomed saucepan. Stir in the oats and salt.

2. Lower the heat and simmer the oatmeal for ten minutes, covered, or until thick and creamy. Stir the oatmeal occasionally while it simmers.

3. Serve the porridge hot in a warm bowl with milk or cream. Some people like a pat of butter melted on top. Sweeten the porridge with treacle, as Mary did, or with white sugar, brown sugar, honey, molasses, or maple syrup. Raisins, dried cranberries, apricots, dates, or other fruits are delicious additions as well.

Makes 1 serving

TREACLE

American readers may not be familiar with treacle, a British syrup made of sugarcane. It is similar to molasses.

There are two types of treacle. Black treacle is a thick, dark, strongly flavored syrup. More popular is the milder treacle known as golden syrup. This is probably the kind of treacle that accompanied Mary's porridge at the manor. It can be found in markets that import British food products, or you can make "American treacle" using the recipe below.

To make American treacle, you will need:

⅓ cup light or mild molasses   *1 tablespoon honey*
⅔ cup white corn syrup

1. Combine the molasses, corn syrup, and honey in a small bowl or pitcher.
2. Mix the ingredients thoroughly.
3. Use the "treacle" as you would molasses or honey.

Makes 1 cup

ORANGE MARMALADE

Marmalade, a sort of jam made of shredded citrus fruit, is a classic British spread for toast, scones, muffins, and crumpets. The cooks at Misselthwaite Manor undoubtedly made marmalade from scratch and stored it in crocks in the pantry. To store your marmalade, you will need to scald a 12-ounce glass jar and lid in boiling water.

To make orange marmalade, you will need:

1 large orange	*Pinch baking soda*
½ cup water	*1½ cups sugar*
1 tablespoon lemon juice	

1. Wash the orange and cut it into fourths.
2. Remove the peel from the orange pieces and scrape away and discard the white pith on the underside of the peels. Cut the orange part of the peels into very fine shreds.
3. Put the orange-peel shreds into a heavy-bottomed saucepan and add the water, lemon juice, and baking soda. Bring the mixture to a boil over medium-high heat, then reduce the heat to a simmer, cover the saucepan, and cook the mixture slowly for ten minutes. Stir occasionally to prevent it from sticking.
4. While the mixture is cooking, chop the orange sections coarsely. Add the chopped orange with its juices to the cooked peel mixture and cook slowly.

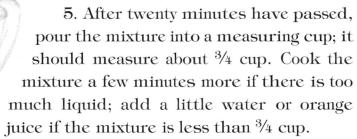

5. After twenty minutes have passed, pour the mixture into a measuring cup; it should measure about ¾ cup. Cook the mixture a few minutes more if there is too much liquid; add a little water or orange juice if the mixture is less than ¾ cup.

6. Return the ¾ cup of the mixture to the saucepan. Add the sugar and stir it in.

7. Bring the mixture to a boil and boil it for five minutes.

8. Remove the marmalade from the heat and let it stand for five minutes; skim off any foam and discard it.

9. Spoon the marmalade into the scalded jar. Cover it and keep it in the refrigerator until you are ready to serve it. The marmalade will keep indefinitely if refrigerated.

Marmalade goes very well with toast. To prepare your toast, place the slices of bread in the toaster or under a heated broiler and toast the bread until it is as brown as you like. Spread the marmalade on the toast and cut into triangles.

Makes 1½ cups

Colin's and Mary's Manor Breakfast

He made up his mind to eat less, but unfortunately it was not possible to carry out this brilliant idea when he wakened each morning with an amazing appetite and the table near his sofa was set with a breakfast of home-made bread and fresh butter, snow-white eggs, raspberry jam and clotted cream.

Both Colin and Mary grew healthier in the fresh air and sunshine of the secret garden, and their appetites improved magnificently. Every morning he and Mary sent their breakfast trays back to the kitchen in a "highly polished condition."

Here is the menu for an elaborate manor-house breakfast such as Mary and Colin enjoyed before going out to the secret garden.

Homemade Bread and Butter

Snow-white Eggs

Raspberry Jam

Clotted Cream

Muffins

Sizzling Ham

HOMEMADE BREAD

At the manor, Mary and Colin could have freshly baked homemade bread every day, thanks to the cook who baked it each morning. Cottage dwellers like Dickon's family set aside a day or two a week for baking enough breads, oatcakes, and other staples to last several days.

Homemade bread is not difficult to make, but it does require time for several risings to ensure that it is light.

To make bread, you will need:

1 cup milk

1 tablespoon sugar

1 teaspoon salt

2 tablespoons shortening, plus extra for greasing the bowl and pan

1¼ teaspoons active dry yeast

3 to 3½ cups sifted all-purpose flour

1 tablespoon melted butter (to brush top of finished loaf)

1. Heat the milk in a small saucepan over low heat until it is lukewarm (110°–115°F if you have a cooking thermometer). Stir in sugar, salt, and shortening (the cooks at the Manor would have used lard).

2. Sprinkle the yeast on top of the warm milk mixture and stir it to dissolve. Set the mixture aside in a warm place for five minutes so the yeast can develop, or until the mixture begins to thicken and bubble.

3. Meanwhile, measure three cups of the flour into a large mixing bowl. Make a little "well" or indentation in the center of the flour.

4. Pour the milk mixture into the well and use a spoon to mix it into the flour.

5. Beat the mixture with the spoon until the batter is smooth, about two minutes.

6. Add more flour, a tablespoon at a time, and mix it in until the dough begins to leave the sides of the bowl.

7. Sprinkle a breadboard, cutting board, or clean countertop with flour and turn the dough onto it.

8. Place the bowl upside down over the dough. Let the dough rest for ten minutes.

9. Flour your hands and knead the dough for eight to ten minutes, until it is smooth and elastic. Form the dough into a ball.

10. Lightly grease a mixing bowl.

11. Place the ball of dough in the bowl and turn it over so that it is lightly greased all over.

12. Cover the bowl with a towel. Set the covered bowl in a warm place and let the dough rise until it is almost double in volume. This will take about one and a half hours.

13. Flour your hand, make a fist, and punch the dough down. Turn it over and let it rise again, covered with the towel, until it is almost double. This will take about forty-five minutes.

14. Turn the dough out onto the floured work surface. Form it into a loaf shape.

15. Grease a loaf pan (9" x 5" x 3") and place the shaped loaf in the pan. Cover the pan with the towel or plastic wrap, set it in a warm place, and let it rise until it is doubled. This will take about an hour.

16. While the loaf is rising, preheat the oven to 400°F. Bake the loaf thirty-five minutes, or until it is golden brown and sounds hollow when tapped lightly with your finger.

17. Wearing oven mitts, remove the bread from the oven. Brush the top with melted butter and remove the loaf from the pan. Cool the loaf on a wire rack. Slice and serve with butter.

Makes 1 loaf

Note: This bread recipe can be doubled to make two loaves. The recipe for one loaf prepares 1 pound of bread dough, so it can also be used to make doughcakes (pages 56–57) and a crusty cottage loaf (page 58). Slices of homemade bread make wonderful toast, too (page 41).

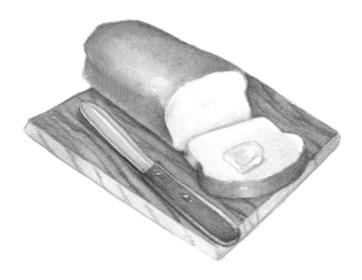

SNOW-WHITE EGGS

Colin and Mary's "snow-white eggs" were probably soft-boiled three-minute eggs, which are typically served in eggcups at breakfast. To eat them, gently crack the top of the egg with the blunt edge of a knife or the back of a teaspoon and cut away enough of the shell so that you can dip a spoon into the egg. It may take practice to avoid letting bits of eggshell drop into the egg!

To cook a soft-boiled egg, you will need:

1 large egg

1. Place the egg in a saucepan and cover it completely with cold water. Set the pan over medium-high heat and bring the water to a boil. When the water begins to boil, simmer for three minutes (four minutes if the egg was cold from the refrigerator).

2. When the time is up, remove the pan from the heat and immediately take the egg out of the water with a spoon. Place the egg on a folded tea towel to dry it, then set it in an eggcup for serving. (If you do not have an eggcup, you can set the egg on a napkin ring to hold it upright or simply lay it in a small saucer or bowl.)

Makes 1 serving

RASPBERRY JAM

The cook at Misselthwaite could make raspberry jam from the fresh berries that grew in the kitchen gardens under the expert care of Ben Weatherstaff.

Raspberries usually ripen in July. They can be made into jam right away, or you can freeze them and make jam later when the weather cools off. To store your jam, you will need to scald an 8-ounce glass jar and lid in boiling water.

To make jam, you will need:

2 cups fresh raspberries　　　　　*1½ cups sugar*
½ apple (optional)

1. Wash the berries well and drain them thoroughly in a colander. Pick out any bruised or discolored berries and discard them.

2. Pour the berries into a heavy-bottomed saucepan. Use a fork to mash some berries to release juice. Peel the apple, cut it into small pieces, and add to the berries. (The apple is optional, but it will help the berries thicken into jam more easily.)

3. Mix the sugar into the berries.

4. Put the pan over medium-low heat and cook the mixture until the sugar dissolves, stirring frequently. Simmer and stir the mixture for about twenty minutes.

5. Drop a spoonful of the hot jam onto a plate; if the jam is thick and doesn't spread out too fast on the plate, it is ready.

6. Carefully pour the jam into the scalded jar. When the jam has cooled, cover it and store it in the refrigerator until you are ready to serve it. Jam will keep indefinitely if refrigerated.

Makes 1 pint

CLOTTED CREAM

Clotted cream (or Devonshire cream) is made from nonhomogenized milk. The milk is heated, then left to stand for several hours or overnight. The thick, heavy cream that rises to the top is scooped off and spread on scones or muffins.

With our store-bought milk, it is nearly impossible to make real clotted cream, but here is how to make a very close cousin to it, if you cannot find the imported variety in specialty food stores.

To make American clotted cream, you will need:

½ pint heavy (whipping) cream   *Dash of salt*
¼ cup dairy sour cream

1. Pour the heavy cream into a mixing bowl and beat with an electric mixer or egg beater until it forms stiff peaks.

2. Stir the sour cream into the whipped cream. Add a dash of salt, if desired.

3. Serve the "clotted cream" with scones or muffins, or over berries for breakfast or teatime.

Makes 1½ cups

MUFFINS

There are two kinds of muffins in England. One kind is made with yeast and baked on a griddle and is similar to a crumpet (pages 62–63). The following kind is more like the muffins Americans are familiar with and is much quicker and easier to make for breakfast or tea.

To make muffins, you will need:

1 egg
½ cup milk
¼ cup vegetable oil
1½ cups flour
½ cup sugar
2 teaspoons baking powder

½ teaspoon salt
1 cup blueberries or other fruit
  (optional)
Butter or other shortening to
  grease muffin pan

1. Preheat the oven to 400°F.
2. Use a fork to blend the egg, milk, and oil in a mixing bowl.
3. Add the flour, sugar, baking powder, and salt. Stir just until the ingredients are mixed; overmixing them will make the muffins tough. Carefully stir in the fruit (optional).
4. Grease a muffin pan and spoon the mixture into its cups, filling them two-thirds full.

5. Bake the muffins twenty to twenty-five minutes. Use oven mitts to remove the muffin pan from the oven.

6. Serve the muffins hot with butter or clotted cream and raspberry jam.

Makes 12 muffins

SIZZLING HAM

Yorkshire is well known for its delicious dry-cured hams. They are salted, smoked, and hung up to cure. This process makes it possible to store the hams without refrigeration, a necessity in Mary's day.

When the cured ham is ready to be cooked, it is soaked in water, then simmered for an hour or two in a large kettle. Next the ham is coated in a mixture of bread crumbs, mustard, treacle, and other delicious ingredients, and baked until it is done.

The ham is sliced and presented on a platter as the main course of a special dinner. Leftover slices are grilled or fried for the next day's breakfast.

To make sizzling ham slices, you will need:

4 ounces sliced cooked ham

1. Place the slices of ham in a cold skillet. Set the skillet over medium-high heat.
2. Cook the ham about two minutes on each side, or until each side is nicely browned. Turn the slices with a cooking fork or spatula.
3. Remove the skillet from the stove onto a heat-proof surface. Arrange the browned, sizzling ham slices on a warm plate and serve.

Makes 1 serving

Tea at the Cottage

"Ask her if you might be driven over to our cottage some day and have a bit o' Mother's hot oat cake, an' butter an' a glass o' milk."

Teatime at the Sowerby cottage would have been quite different from teatime at the manor. The menu would have consisted of sturdy, filling, country-style foods instead of dainty sandwiches and cakes. Tea would be served outside or inside at the rustic table the family used. Here are some ideas for a cottage-style afternoon tea such as one the Sowerbys might have prepared for Mary and Colin.

Mother's Hot Oatcake

Martha's Doughcakes

Crusty Cottage Loaf

Cottage Apple Crumble

Milk

Tea

MOTHER'S HOT OATCAKE

Oatcake, also known in Yorkshire as haverbread or havercake, is different from the oatcakes the children ate for their woodland tea (page 72). This oatcake is made with a yeast batter and baked on a griddle or in the oven.

In Yorkshire cottages like the Sowerbys', oatcake was on hand at all times. On baking day it was made in large quantities, and some was eaten fresh from the fire while it was soft. Extra loaves were hung over cords or dowels near the ceiling of the cottage so they would dry and become crisp. They were then eaten during the week.

To make Mrs. Sowerby's hot oatcake, you will need:

1 cup milk	*1½ cups finely ground oatmeal*
1 cup water	*½ cup whole wheat flour*
1 ounce fresh yeast (or 2¼	*1 teaspoon salt*
teaspoons active dry yeast	*2 teaspoons shortening (for*
and 1 teaspoon sugar)	*greasing the griddle)*

1. In a saucepan, mix the milk and water. Set the saucepan over low heat until the mixture is lukewarm to the touch, or 110°F if you are using a cooking thermometer.

2. Pour the warmed mixture into a large mixing bowl. Crumble the fresh yeast into the warm milk and water and stir it until it is dissolved. If you are using dry yeast, stir it and the sugar into the warm liquid and set it aside in a warm place for about five minutes, or until the mixture begins to thicken and bubble, before proceeding.

3. Stir the oatmeal, flour, and salt into the milk and yeast mixture. Add more warm water, if necessary, to make a batter. Cover the bowl

with a damp towel or plastic wrap and set it aside in a warm place for about an hour.

4. Lightly grease a griddle or large skillet and place it over medium heat.

5. Stir the oatcake batter and spoon about ⅔ cup of it into the hot pan, spreading it slightly to make a thin oval cake in the middle of the pan.

6. Cook the oatcake for just a few minutes, until it is set but not browned on the bottom. Turn the oatcake and cook it briefly on the other side. (Repeat procedure until batter is used up.)

7. Serve the oatcake hot, letting each person break off a piece for herself. Spread the oatcake with butter and jam or marmalade, if desired. Dry any leftover loaves of oatcake on a wire rack, store them covered, and eat them later, plain or with cheese.

Makes 6 oatcakes

MARTHA'S DOUGHCAKES

Using leftover bread dough from the day's baking, Martha made individual doughcakes for the children. She probably baked them on a griddle over the open fire while the cottage loaves baked in the oven. The middles of the doughcakes were left a bit underdone or "doughy" in the middle to live up to their name.

To make Martha's doughcakes, you will need:

1 pound prepared bread dough
    (see pages 43–45)
2 tablespoons butter or other
    shortening

¼ cup brown sugar
Flour for work surface

1. Divide the bread dough into twelve equal pieces and flatten them slightly with your hand.

2. Spread a little butter on each piece of dough and put a teaspoon of brown sugar in the middle of each one.

3. Draw the edges of the rounds of dough together over the brown sugar and press them together so that the sugar is enclosed in the center of the dough.

4. Flatten the rounds with your hand again and place them on a floured board or counter. Cover the rounds with a damp towel or plastic wrap and let them rise for thirty minutes.

5. Heat the griddle over medium-high heat. Melt a teaspoonful of butter on the hot griddle, and when it begins to sizzle, put two or three of the doughcakes on the griddle.

6. Cook the doughcakes on each side until they are golden brown (about four or five minutes each).

7. While you cook the remaining cakes, add more butter to the griddle as necessary to keep the dough from sticking.

8. Serve the doughcakes warm with butter. Sprinkle with a little more brown sugar, if desired.

Makes 12 doughcakes

CRUSTY COTTAGE LOAF

Yorkshire cottage loaf is the name given to a round loaf of bread with a little ball on top.

To make a crusty cottage loaf, you will need:

1 tablespoon butter or other
    shortening
2 tablespoons flour or cornmeal

1 pound bread dough (see
    pages 43–45)

1. Preheat the oven to 400°F.

2. Grease a baking sheet and sprinkle it with flour or cornmeal.

3. Cut one fourth of the bread dough away from the full loaf. Shape it into a ball and set it aside.

4. Form the remaining dough into a large round. Place it on the baking sheet. Make a shallow depression in the center of the dough with your fingers and place the smaller ball of dough in the depression.

5. Bake the loaf in the preheated oven for thirty-five minutes, or until it is golden brown. Wearing oven mitts, remove the sheet from the oven.

6. Cool the cottage loaf on a wire rack. When you are ready to serve it, cut the loaf into slices.

Makes 1 loaf

COTTAGE APPLE CRUMBLE

Apple crumble is a delicious and filling dessert, popular throughout Yorkshire.

Mary and Colin and Dickon could have picked a basketful of apples that grew on trees trained along the south-facing wall of the secret garden or in the orchards nearby.

To make cottage apple crumble, you will need:

⅓ cup flour
⅓ cup finely ground oatmeal
½ teaspoon ground cinnamon
¼ teaspoon ginger
¼ teaspoon cloves
4 tablespoons butter plus a bit more for greasing the baking dish

⅓ cup brown sugar
2 large cooking apples (such as Granny Smith)
1 lemon
2 tablespoons orange marmalade (see recipe page 40)

1. Preheat oven to 375°F.
2. Mix the flour, oatmeal, and spices in a medium-size bowl.
3. Cut three tablespoons of the butter into small pieces and add them to the flour mixture. Cut the butter into the flour with a fork or pastry cutter until the mixture resembles coarse meal or breadcrumbs.
4. Mix in the brown sugar. Set the mixture aside.
5. Core, peel, and thinly slice the apples. Place them in a large bowl.
6. Grate the yellow part of the lemon rind and add it to the apples.

7. Cut the lemon in half, squeeze the juice, and add it to the apples. Add the marmalade. Mix well.

8. Grease a one-quart baking dish.

9. Put half the sliced apples into the baking dish; spoon half the flour/oat mixture evenly over the apples. Repeat with remaining apples and flour/oat mixture.

10. Cut the remaining tablespoon of butter into small pieces and scatter them over the top.

11. Bake the crumble for forty-five minutes to one hour, or until the apples are tender and the topping is crunchy. Wearing oven mitts, remove it from the oven to a wire rack and let it cool for about ten minutes.

12. Serve the apple crumble warm. It is delicious accompanied by a slice of cheddar cheese, thick cream, or sweetened whipped cream, if desired.

Makes 6 servings

Afternoon Tea in the Garden

It was an agreeable idea, easily carried out, and when the white cloth was spread upon the grass, with hot tea and buttered toast and crumpets, a delightfully hungry meal was eaten.

Afternoon tea in a secret garden was especially appealing for Colin, Dickon, and Mary on Colin's first day out in the fresh air in the secret garden. The garden worked its magic on Colin as it had on Mary. His color improved, his appetite awakened, and he sent Mary to tell the servants to bring afternoon tea outside.

Once Dickon's mother, Mrs. Sowerby, sent over two pails of "rich new milk with cream on the top of it" and "cottage-made currant buns folded in a clean blue and white napkin." Another time she "packed a basket which held a regular feast" which may have included some of these delicious treats.

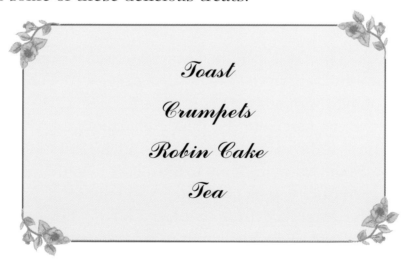

Toast

Crumpets

Robin Cake

Tea

(Description for toast is on page 41)

CRUMPETS

At the first secret garden afternoon tea, Dickon's black crow, Soot, "took the entire half of a buttered crumpet into a corner and pecked at and examined and turned it over and made hoarse remarks about it until he decided to swallow it all joyfully in one gulp."

Teatime manners dictate that crumpets be nibbled a bit more daintily than Soot demonstrated that afternoon. But crumpets are so tasty that sometimes it is hard to remember good manners!

To make crumpets, you will need:

¼ cup water	1½ cups flour
½ cup milk	¼ teaspoon salt
½ ounce fresh yeast (or 1	2 tablespoons butter
teaspoon active dry yeast	OPTIONAL:
and ½ teaspoon sugar)	Butter and jam
1 egg	

1. Mix the water and milk in a saucepan, set it over medium heat, and heat the mixture until it is lukewarm (or 110°–115°F. if you are using a cooking thermometer).

2. Remove the pan from the heat and crumble in the fresh yeast, stirring it until it dissolves. If you are using dry yeast, sprinkle it and the sugar into the warm milk mixture and set it aside for five minutes, or until the mixture begins to thicken and bubble.

3. Pour the yeast mixture into a large mixing bowl and stir in the egg, flour, and salt. Beat the mixture heartily with a wooden spoon until it is smooth. (The more you beat it, the more holes will form in the finished crumpets.)

4. Cover the bowl with a towel or plastic wrap and set the mixture aside in a warm place for about one and a half hours, or until it has doubled in bulk.

5. When the mixture is ready, heat a griddle or skillet over medium heat. Melt the butter on the griddle and set as many muffin rings on the griddle as will fit comfortably.

6. Drop a spoonful of batter into each ring. When bubbles form and break on top and the bottoms are golden brown, take the muffin rings off (using oven mitts). Slip a spatula under each crumpet, turn it, and cook it briefly on the other side. Repeat with the remaining batter.

7. Serve the crumpets hot from the griddle with plenty of butter and jam, if desired. Leftover crumpets can be cooled on a rack and toasted later.

Makes 12 crumpets

ROBIN CAKE

Robin cake was popular at the huge teas that followed the miners' annual festivals in the coal-mining areas of Yorkshire. It is a rather flat, dense cake, not too sweet. In honor of Mary's friendly robin that led her into the secret garden, it seems especially appropriate to include the recipe here. Perhaps you will leave a few crumbs for the robins and other birds in your garden after you have finished your tea.

To make robin cake, you will need:

1½ cups flour
½ cup finely ground oatmeal
⅓ cup granulated sugar
1 teaspoon ground ginger
½ teaspoon ground nutmeg
1 teaspoon baking soda
¼ cup butter
¼ cup shortening, plus extra for greasing pan

3 tablespoons milk
2 tablespoons black treacle (see page 39) or dark molasses
1 egg, beaten
2 tablespoons confectioners' sugar (optional)

1. Preheat the oven to 400°F.

2. Mix the dry ingredients (flour, oatmeal, sugar, spices, and baking soda) in a large bowl.

3. Add the butter and shortening to the dry ingredients and blend them with your fingers (or a pastry blender, if you prefer) until they are well mixed.

4. Stir the milk and treacle together in a small saucepan and heat them just until the treacle dissolves and the mixture is warm.

5. Pour the milk mixture into the dry ingredients and mix them with a spoon until a stiff dough forms. Add the egg and mix thoroughly.

6. Turn the dough into a 9" x 9" greased baking tin and spread it out evenly.

7. Bake the cake in the preheated oven about thirty minutes, or until it is golden brown.

8. Wearing oven mitts, remove the cake from the oven. Cool the cake in the pan and cut it into squares to serve.

9. Pour the confectioners' sugar into a strainer and sift it over the top of the cooled cake, if desired, to add a special teatime touch to the finished cake.

Makes 9 servings

A Woodland Tea

You can trifle with your breakfast and seem to disdain your dinner if you are full to the brim with roasted eggs and potatoes and richly frothed new milk and oat cakes and buns and heather honey and clotted cream.

Occasionally Dickon, Mary, and Colin ventured for walks in the forested park surrounding the manor house. They roasted eggs and potatoes for their afternoon tea in an oven made of stones that were heated by the small fire they built inside it.

Clotted Cream

Heather Honey

Roasted Eggs

Roasted Potatoes

Oatcakes

Cottage-made Currant Buns

Tea

CLOTTED CREAM
(Recipe for clotted cream is on page 49.)

HEATHER HONEY

The heather honey the children enjoyed was honey the bees had made from the heather that bloomed on the moors. If you are not fortunate enough to find a jar of heather honey, you can surely find a jar of clover honey, apple-blossom honey, or any number of other honeys made from the nectars of different flowers.

ROASTED EGGS

If you are cooking outside, make an oven of stones as Dickon, Colin, and Mary did by digging a shallow hole in the dirt and lining it with stones. With adult supervision, build a small wood or charcoal fire and let it burn down until there are just hot coals left. With a long-handled fire poker or other fireproof tool, spread the coals out into a single layer. Carefully place wrapped eggs (see below) on the coals and ashes. Rake some of the coals over the tops of the wrapped eggs. Cover the fire pit with a few large flat stones to hold the heat in.

To make roasted eggs in your outdoor oven, you will need:

18–24 large green leaves (such as grape or maple leaves)
6 green vines stripped of leaves, each about 2' long, or twine

6 large eggs
Salt and pepper

1. Soak the leaves and vines in a pan or bucket of water for about ten minutes.

2. Pierce each end of the shell of each egg with a skewer or needle to allow air to escape during cooking.

3. Wrap each egg in several layers of green leaves. Tie the leaves around each egg with a piece of vine.

4. Roast the egg packages in your outdoor stone oven for twenty minutes (instructions for roasting above).

5. Remove the eggs from the stone oven with tongs. Wear oven mitts for extra protection.

6. Shell the eggs, sprinkle them with salt and pepper, and eat them as you would hard-boiled eggs.

Makes 6 servings

Note: There is another, simpler version of roasted eggs you can make indoors. Just roll shelled, hard-boiled eggs in melted butter, sprinkle them with salt and pepper, and place them in a skillet. Place the pan over medium heat and brown all sides of the eggs slightly. Serve the eggs hot.

ROASTED POTATOES

The children roasted potatoes in the woodland stone oven along with the eggs. With a generous helping of butter and a sprinkling of salt and pepper, they found them "fit for a woodland king—besides being deliciously satisfying."

To make roasted potatoes, you will need:

6 potatoes	*Salt*
Vegetable oil or shortening	*Butter*

1. Wash the potatoes and rub them all over with a generous coating of oil or shortening.

2. Prick the skin of each potato in several places with a fork.

3. Carefully lay the potatoes in the hot coals of the outdoor stone oven and roast them as you did the roasted eggs (page 68). The potatoes should be done in about thirty to forty-five minutes. (To test the potatoes for doneness, pierce them with a fork. If the fork goes into the center of the potato easily, the potato is done.)

4. Wearing oven mitts, remove the potatoes from the stone oven with tongs. Tap the potatoes gently on a rock to knock off most of the ashes.

5. Cut the potatoes in half and top them with butter, salt, and pepper. Eat the inside of the potato, not the charred outside.

Makes 6 servings

Note: You can roast potatoes in your kitchen oven, too. Preheat the oven to 400°F and prepare the potatoes according to steps 1 and 2 above. Place the prepared potatoes in the hot oven, using oven mitts to protect your hands. Cook them for an hour, test them for doneness (as in step 4 above), and remove them from the oven. Serve the potatoes hot. When roasted in your kitchen oven, the skins of the potatoes may be eaten.

OATCAKES

Oatcakes, a traditional Yorkshire treat, are almost like crackers. They are thin and flat, delicious plain or topped with butter or cheese.

To make oatcakes, you will need:

1¼ cups finely ground oatmeal *1 teaspoon sugar (optional)*
¼ teaspoon baking powder *1 tablespoon melted butter*
¼ teaspoon salt *¼ cup boiling water*

1. Preheat oven to 300°F.

2. Mix the oatmeal, baking powder, salt, and sugar (if desired) in a large bowl.

3. Stir in the melted butter and boiling water.

4. After the mixture has slightly cooled, lightly knead the dough with greased hands—in the bowl or on a board lightly sprinked with oatmeal—just until it forms a smooth ball.

5. Sprinkle a flat surface with more oatmeal and roll out the dough with a rolling pin as thinly as possible in a circle, pinching the breaking edges back together with your fingers as necessary.

6. Lift the round onto a baking sheet and cut it into eight pie-shaped pieces.

7. Bake the oatcakes in the preheated oven for twenty minutes.

8. Remove the oatcakes from the oven using oven mitts and cool them on a wire rack.

Makes 8 oatcakes

COTTAGE-MADE CURRANT BUNS

Sometimes currant buns were made from yeast-bread dough on baking day, but on other days, this quick, very rich version would be made.

They are delicious with a cup of tea. They are so rich, they do not need any extra butter!

To make cottage-made currant buns, you will need:

2½ cups flour
2 tablespoons baking powder
1 teaspoon salt
8 tablespoons butter

¼ cup dried currants
1 cup milk
¼ cup sugar (optional)

1. Preheat the oven to 400°F.
2. Sift the flour, baking powder, and salt together into a large bowl.

3. Cut the butter into small pieces and add to the flour mixture. With a pastry blender or a fork, mix the butter into the flour mixture until it is the texture of coarse meal.

4. Stir in the currants. Add the milk and stir it in until a firm dough forms.

5. Divide the dough into twelve pieces. Roll each piece into a ball and place it on a baking sheet.

6. Flatten the buns slightly with your hand. They should be about one inch thick.

7. Sprinkle a little sugar on top of each bun, if desired.

8. Bake the buns in the preheated oven for twelve to fifteen minutes, or until golden brown. Wear oven mitts to remove the baking sheet from the oven.

9. Serve the buns warm, "folded in a clean blue and white napkin," as Mrs. Sowerby did, if desired.

Makes 12 buns

Chapter Four

In the Garden:
Ideas for Creating Your
Own Secret Gardens

"Might I," quavered Mary, "might I have a bit of earth?"

*T*he secret garden on the vast grounds of gloomy Misselthwaite Manor had been neglected for over ten years. But when Mary Lennox, herself lonely and neglected, unlocked the secret garden and lovingly began to restore it, wonderful things happened. As the garden bloomed with flowers, Mary began to bloom with purpose and confidence. Colin, crippled in mind and body from years of imagined illness, also bloomed with health and hope as he worked in the garden. Both Mary and Colin grew in many ways as they tended their "bit of earth."

Not all of us have at our disposal an entire large, walled private kingdom as the secret garden was at first for Mary, Colin, and Dickon. We can, however, create our own special places to provide us with the same magical feelings of delight and satisfaction as the secret garden provided its gardeners.

If you would like to tend your own "bit of earth," here are some ideas and instructions for several different "secret gardens"—on a smaller scale, of course!

A SPRING BULB GARDEN

"They're bulbs," answered Martha. "Lots o' spring flowers grow from 'em. Th' very little ones are snowdrops an' crocuses an' th' big ones are narcissuses an' jonquils an' daffydowndillies. The biggest of all is lilies an' purple flags."

Mary thought the strange little knobs she found in the secret garden looked like onions, and they do! Planted in the fall, bulbs start growing roots and get ready to push through the soil in early spring. The smallest bulbs usually bloom first, the larger ones later. Some bulbs, such as lilies, bloom in summer.

Planting bulbs is a wonderful way to start creating your own version of the secret garden. You can even plant bulbs in pots if you prefer.

To plant a small bulb garden with the same kinds of bulbs found in the secret garden, you will need:

Shovel or garden fork　　　　　*3 dozen jonquil bulbs*
Wheelbarrow or ground cloth　　*3 dozen narcissus bulbs*
Topsoil, compost, manure, peat　*3 dozen Dutch iris bulbs*
　moss (optional)　　　　　　　　*("flags")*
Bulb fertilizer　　　　　　　　　*5 dozen snowdrop bulbs*
12–15 tiger lily bulbs or 4　　　*5 dozen crocus bulbs*
　daylily plants　　　　　　　　　*Dry leaves or hay*
3 dozen daffodil bulbs　　　　　*Rake*

1. In your garden select a sunny spot about three feet in diameter.

2. With a shovel or garden fork, dig down into the earth, loosening it up and removing any roots, stones, or other material that would

interfere with the growing bulbs. Cultivate the dirt to at least eighteen inches below ground level. Remove most of the dirt from the hole and pile it in a wheelbarrow or on a ground cloth next to the hole.

3. If necessary, add a few shovelfuls of topsoil, compost, manure, or peat moss to enrich the soil and lighten it to make it easier for the bulbs to grow.

4. Mix in some bulb fertilizer according to the package directions.

5. Begin to plant the bulbs, starting with the largest ones. Be sure to plant the pointed end up and the root end down. Place the larger bulbs, such as daffodils, lilies, and jonquils, in the bottom of the hole, about four inches apart. Cover them carefully with dirt from the wheelbarrow, just until they are barely covered.

6. Plant a layer of medium-size bulbs, such as narcissuses, smaller daffodils, and Dutch irises, above and adjacent to the first layer of bulbs (see diagram), and cover them with dirt as you did before.

7. Finally, plant a thick layer of snowdrops and crocuses, about an inch apart, and cover them with dirt. Press the dirt down gently but firmly.

8. Water the plot well and cover it with a thick layer of dry leaves or hay to insulate it for winter. Carefully rake this away in the spring as the tips of the plants begin to show.

9. Water the bulbs during the spring if it doesn't rain regularly and the soil is dry.

10. After the flowers in the bulb garden bloom, cut off the stems and dead flowers but let the green leaves remain. They will provide food for the bulbs so they will bloom again the following spring.

SECRET GARDEN
IN A FLOWERPOT

"How'd tha' like to plant a bit o' somethin'? I can get thee a rose in a pot."

The greenhouse at Misselthwaite Manor was filled with all sorts of plants. Some were seedlings that were started in the winter months, and some were plants that were brought in from the garden for the winter. The glass walls and roof of the greenhouse kept the plants from freezing and provided sunlight to help them grow. The gardeners could water the plants and care for them throughout the winter. When spring came, the plants could be planted outside in the ground or in large urns or planters.

Even if you just have a tiny space for plants, you can make your own secret garden in a flowerpot or urn.

You will need:

1 quart gravel
1 large flowerpot or urn, 12–18"
in diameter (see pages
91–92 for instructions on
making a moss-covered urn
like the ones in the secret
garden)

5–10 pounds potting soil
1 potted miniature rosebush
3 potted ivy plants
Trowel

1. Pour the gravel an inch deep into the bottom of the pot.
2. Fill two thirds of the pot with potting soil.

3. Remove the rosebush from its container and place it in the center of the pot, on top of the soil.

4. Remove the ivy plants from their containers and place them around the rosebush near the edges of the pot as shown. Adjust the plants so that they are evenly spaced.

5. With the trowel, add more potting soil to the pot, filling in around the plants. Press the soil down firmly to hold the plants in place.

6. Water the plants well. Add more soil if necessary.

7. Set the pot in a spot where it will receive plenty of sunshine, and check the pot every day to see if it needs water.

AN INDOOR SECRET GARDEN

"I can have my garden!" cried Mary. "I may have it where I like!"

You can have a tiny secret garden all your own—indoors!

To make your own indoor secret garden, you will need:

1–2 quarts gravel or sand
1 metal pan or plastic tray
*   (12" x 17")*
11 4" terra-cotta tiles
4 2" pots of flowers (such as
*   violets or pansies) or green*
*   plants (such as baby's tears*
*   or ivy)*
1 bag green sheet moss
*   (available at florists' shops)*

OPTIONAL:
4 3–4" pots of ivy
20–24" florists' wire or a coat
*   hanger*
Coated wire or string
2 empty flowerpots
2 3–4" pots of miniature
*   treelike plants (such as*
*   small palms or evergreens)*
1 4" pot snowdrops or crocuses
*   (in spring), miniature roses*
*   (in summer), or dwarf*
*   marigolds (in autumn)*
Eggcups, flat stones or bark,
*   miniature animals, miniature*
*   tea set, scrap of cloth, tiny*
*   robin, tiny key, and other*
*   decorative accessories*

1. Pour a half-inch layer of gravel into the pan. Erect a "wall" by arranging a row of terra-cotta tiles around the edges of the pan, leaving an opening at one end (the entrance to the garden).

2. Set the four two-inch pots of flowers or green plants in the center of the tray; arrange pieces of green sheet moss from the florist in between to form "paths" and to help hide the pots' edges. This will form the centerpiece of your miniature secret garden. You can stop here if you want, or finish the rest of the activity to make a more elaborate indoor garden.

OPTIONAL:

3. Surround the entire garden with larger pots of ivy, perhaps just one on each corner. Intertwine the tendrils of ivy so that they suggest an ivy-covered wall around the garden.

4. Make an arch of ivy to form a little gateway into the garden. Bend the length of thin florist's wire and insert one end into one pot of ivy, the other into a second pot of ivy. Each pot should stand on one side of the opening in the tile "wall." Weave one of the longer vines of ivy from each pot up and around the wire until they meet at the top, forming an ivy-covered arch. Secure the tendrils with a bit of coated wire or string, if necessary.

5. To make "trees," turn two empty flowerpots upside down and set them at the two far corners of

the garden. Set a potted treelike plant on top of each one.

6. For extra color, set a small pot of snowdrops or crocuses, a miniature rose, or dwarf marigolds in the center of the garden. (You could substitute dried or silk flowers if you prefer.)

7. Furnish your secret garden with "urns" (eggcups are ideal), benches (make them with flat stones or bits of bark), and a tiny sundial (a button set upon a stick would be perfect). If you have some tiny toy animals, place a few among the plants or near a bench. A tiny robin set in one of the plants would add a special touch, along with a tiny key near the ivy arch and a miniature tea set or picnic basket placed near one of the trees.

8. No matter what you plant in your indoor secret garden, be sure to care for it as tenderly as Mary did her larger one. Water the plants before they dry out (twice a week should be about right for the smallest pots, once a week for the larger ones) and give them plenty of light. You may even find yourself talking and whistling to them once in a while as Dickon did!

Chapter Five

Garden Crafts and Skipping Rope

The next day the rain poured down in torrents again, and when Mary looked out of her window the moor was almost hidden by gray mist and cloud. There could be no going out today.

Mary and Colin and Dickon spent every sunny day in the secret garden, pruning or weeding or simply enjoying the garden and the fresh air. Often, though, the weather wasn't suitable for going out to the garden. Even in summer, England is famous for its rainy days.

Dickon was never at a loss for something to do, for he liked to ramble over the moors even in the rain. Mary and Colin, however, had to learn to amuse themselves.

Martha introduced Mary to the joys of skipping rope. And after Mary and Colin discovered the secret garden, they spent many rainy days looking at gardening books.

In this chapter, you will find many activities inspired by *The Secret Garden* that you can do both indoors and out, from skipping rope to pressing flowers to making a nest-building station for robins and other birds that live near your garden.

TWIG TOOL HOLDER

He showed her how to use the fork while he dug about roots with the spade. . . .

When you have finished gardening, you should always brush the dirt from your tools, wipe them with a bit of oil to keep them from rusting, and put them away in a holder or on a rack.

You can make a simple rack to keep your small hand tools easy to find. Use a tree branch you find on the ground or one that has already been pruned from a tree.

To make a twig tool holder, you will need:

1 sturdy tree branch, at least 1½" in diameter and at least 18" long
Pruning scissors
3–6 cup hooks (optional)

1 yard raffia, twine, leather lacing, or dried grapevine (Raffia, long strands of dry palm leaves, can be bought in bundles in craft stores.)

1. Decide which side of the branch will be the front side (the side where your tools will hang).

2. Trim any twigs on the front of the branch to about two inches long with the pruning scissors. You can hang some of your tools from these "hooks." Trim all the other twigs on the branch as close to the branch as possible.

3. Screw in a few cup hooks to add hanging spaces for more tools.

88

4. Tie one end of the raffia (or other hanging material) about an inch from one end of the branch. Tie the other end of the raffia to the other end of the branch.

5. Hang the branch on a hook at the center of the raffia hanger. Adjust the length of the hanger if necessary by retying one end and cutting off any excess.

6. Hang your tools on the twig hooks and cup hooks where they will be handy for using in your garden. (If necessary, tie a piece of leather lacing or cord through the handles of the tools to serve as loops for hanging.)

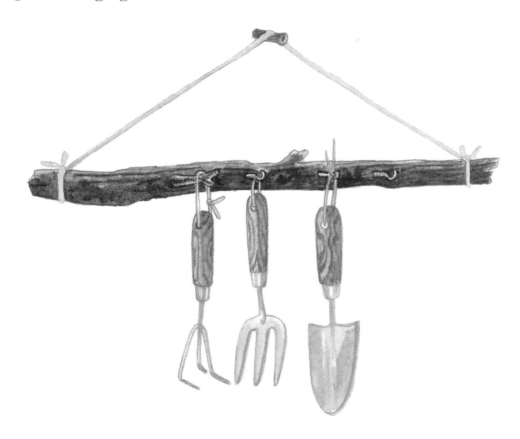

PLANT LABELS

"I couldna' say that there name," he said, pointing to one under which was written "Aquilegia," "but us calls that a columbine. . . ."

There are many ways to make signs for the plants in your garden. Here is an idea for using ordinary materials as identification labels.

To make plant labels, you will need:

Rocks or bricks	*Acrylic paints in your choice*
Pencil	*of colors*
Small paintbrushes	*Cups of water for cleaning*
	brushes

1. Make a list of the names of the plants in your garden.
2. Choose a rock or brick for each plant.
3. With a pencil, neatly print the name of one plant on each rock.
4. With the paintbrush and paints, paint over the penciled names. If you like, paint a simple picture of the flower you have named on the same rock.
5. Set the painted rocks in front of the plants they identify.

MOSS-COVERED FLOWER URNS

There seemed to have been grass paths here and there, and in one or two corners there were alcoves of evergreen with stone seats or tall moss-covered flower urns in them.

The urns in the secret garden had become covered with moss during the many years that the garden had been untended. Just about any pot made of porous materials like stone or terra-cotta or even concrete will eventually develop a coat of moss if left outside for a long period of time. However, there is a method to speed the process along if you wish.

To make a moss-covered flower urn, you will need:

1 terra-cotta, stone, or concrete pot

Old newspapers

1 tablespoon moss (scrape up some moss already growing on a stone or on the ground)

1 cup buttermilk or plain yogurt

1 Popsicle stick or other stirring stick

1 large paintbrush

1. Place the pot upside down on a flat surface covered with newspaper.

2. Crumble the moss into the buttermilk or yogurt. Stir.

3. Dip the paintbrush into the mixture. Brush it on the outside of the pot.

4. Place the pot in a dark place for about a week. Moss will start to grow on the sides of the pot.

5. Fill the pot with potting soil and plant it with your favorite flowers.

KEY WIND CHIMES

It was something like a ring of rusty iron or brass and when the robin flew up into a tree nearby she put out her hand and picked the ring up. It was more than a ring, however; it was an old key which looked as if it had been buried a long time.

The key that the robin found led Mary to the gate to the secret garden.

To create a keepsake you can hang in your own garden or on a tree branch, make a set of wind chimes using interesting old keys.

To make key wind chimes, you will need:

2 6"-long sticks, about ½" in diameter (Twigs are ideal, but you can use Popsicle sticks, dowels, or chopsticks, too.)

1 36" length of twine
5 old keys, each at least 1½" long
5 18" lengths of twine

1. Place the two sticks side by side and tie them together in the middle with the long piece of twine.

2. Spread the sticks apart into an X shape and wrap the ends of the twine four or five times around the junction of the sticks in figure-eight fashion to hold the sticks securely. Tie a tight knot to hold the twine in place. Leave the ends of the twine loose.

3. Tie each key to one end of each of the five eighteen-inch lengths of twine.

4. Tie the other ends of the twine pieces to the X frame, one in the center and one about a half inch from the end of each of the sticks as shown.

5. Hang the wind chime on the branch of a tree, tying the loose ends over the desired position.

WATERING CAN PLANTER

Mary slipped out to run and bring back a watering-can.

A watering can is good for watering plants in pots and for watering seedlings. It also makes a fine planter for the porch or for a spot in the garden. Today watering cans are often made of heavy plastic, but you can still find metal ones such as Mary would have used in the secret garden.

To make a watering can planter, you will need:

1 quart stones or gravel
1 watering can
1 gallon potting soil
Trowel

Miniature rosebush or other
  flowering plant
2 4" pots of ivy or other
  trailing plants

1. Pour the stones into the watering can. They should cover the bottom of the can and be at least two or three inches deep.

2. Use the trowel to scoop potting soil into the watering can until it is about two inches from the top.

3. With the trowel, dig a space for the miniature rosebush (or other flowering plant).

4. Remove the rosebush from its pot and place it in the hole you have dug in the can.

5. Dig a small hole for each of the ivy plants on either side of the rosebush. Place the ivy plants in the can.

6. Scoop more potting soil around the plants and press it down gently but firmly to hold the plants in place.

7. Place the watering can planter in a sunny location.

8. Water the plants daily or as needed.

TWIG TRELLIS

He stepped over to the nearest tree—an old, old one with gray lichen all over its bark, but upholding a curtain of tangled sprays and branches.

In most gardens, a trellis is a frame built of strips of wood to support climbing plants. The old tree in the secret garden was a sort of natural trellis, providing the ideal support for the climbing roses and vines to grow on.

A trellis can be substantial enough to set in the ground for large, heavy vines to grow over, or it can be small enough to fit into a potted plant or urn.

To make a small twig trellis, you will need:

2 long twigs, at least ½" in diameter and 18" long
Ruler
3 shorter twigs, at least ½" in diameter and 10" long

6 12" pieces brown jute twine or raffia strips (available in craft stores)

1. Lay the two long twigs side by side on a flat surface, about eight inches apart.
2. Lay the three shorter twigs across the long twigs, starting about an inch from the top. The second twig should be about four inches below the top twig, and the third one four inches down from the second one. The ends of the twigs should stick out about one inch on either side of the long support twigs.

3. Wind a piece of twine or raffia in a figure-eight pattern around each of the joining points of the twigs as shown, leaving about three inches of twine at each end for tying a knot. (Wetting the twine or raffia first may make it easier to work with and will make the join tighter when it dries.)

4. Once the three short twigs are tied to the two long ones, check the trellis to see if it is secure. If not, retie the twine as needed.

5. Clip the ends of the twine close to the knots.

6. Stick the long ends of the trellis into a pot or the ground. It can simply be a decoration for a planter, or it can be useful for vine plants (such as morning glories, sweet peas, or ivy) to climb over.

Note: For a larger trellis, use longer, thicker twigs or branches.

Flower Activities

PRESSED FLOWERS

Pick the prettiest ones. . . .

If Mary and Colin and Dickon had not been so busy working in the secret garden all spring and summer, they might have thought of pressing some of the pretty flowers and leaves to look at through the winter months when the garden would be "wick" but resting. Pressing flowers was a very popular hobby in Victorian times. The pressed flowers were carefully arranged in elaborate designs on fine paper and framed or placed in scrapbooks.

It is easy to press flowers and leaves from your garden. They make beautiful decorations for greeting cards, place cards, bookmarks, and many other things. They also provide a record of the kinds of plants that you have planted in your garden from year to year if you keep samples of them in a flower scrapbook (page 101).

To press flowers, you will need:

A thick, old telephone book or dictionary
Fresh flowers and leaves (Flat leaves and easy-to-flatten flowers such as pansies, daisies, and violets work best. You can also gently pull petals from more complex flowers such as roses, marigolds, and geraniums and press the petals individually.)
3 or 4 heavy books
Tray or newspapers
Wax paper (optional)

1. Open the telephone book or dictionary.

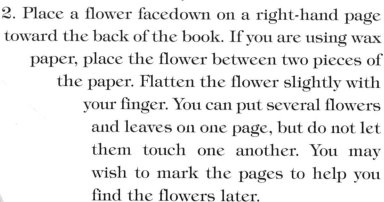

2. Place a flower facedown on a right-hand page toward the back of the book. If you are using wax paper, place the flower between two pieces of the paper. Flatten the flower slightly with your finger. You can put several flowers and leaves on one page, but do not let them touch one another. You may wish to mark the pages to help you find the flowers later.

3. Carefully turn several of the left-hand pages over the flowers and leaves. Add more flowers to another page of the telephone book.

4. Continue steps 2 and 3 until you have all your flowers pressed.

5. Close the book and stack several heavy books, such as encyclopedia volumes, on top of it.

6. Wait at least a week before removing the heavy books and opening the telephone book.

7. Carefully open the telephone book to the pages where you put flowers. They should be flat and dry by now. Gently remove them to a tray or flat newspaper.

8. The pressed flowers are ready to use as you wish.

PRESSED FLOWER SCRAPBOOK

They looked at pictures in the gardening books and Dickon knew all the flowers by their country names and knew exactly which ones were already growing in the secret garden.

As a reminder of your garden and a reference for future planting, compile a scrapbook featuring samples of flowers and leaves from your garden along with information and observations about them. You can buy a scrapbook or make your own.

To make a flower scrapbook, you will need:

12 or more 8½" x 11" pieces of watercolor paper

12 or more 8½" x 11" pieces of onionskin paper

Ruler

Hole punch

2 9" x 12" pieces heavy cardboard

2 11" x 14" sheets of decorative paper

2 9" x 12" sheets of decorative paper

Craft glue or spray adhesive

Raffia or ribbon

Pressed flowers (see pages 99–100)

1. Stack the paper, alternating a piece of watercolor paper with a piece of onion-skin paper. These will be the pages of your scrapbook.

2. Punch two holes in the left side of the pages half an inch in from the left edge, one hole two inches from the top and one hole two inches from the bottom. Set the pages aside.

3. To make the cover of the scrapbook, place the two pieces of nine-by-twelve-inch cardboard on a flat surface.

4. Center one piece of cardboard on each piece of the eleven-by-fourteen-inch paper. Glue the paper to the cardboard. Clip the corners of the paper and fold the edges over to the back of the cardboard. Smooth the paper over the front and on the back edges.

5. Glue the nine-by-twelve-inch pieces of paper onto the backs of the cardboard, covering the folded-down edges of the front papers.

6. Punch holes in the left side of the covers to match the holes in the pages (half an inch in from the left edge, one hole two and a half inches down from the top and one hole two and a half inches up from the bottom).

7. Place the stack of watercolor and onionskin paper on top of the back side of one of the cardboard covers. Place the other cardboard cover on top of this stack with the front side facing out. Line up the holes.

8. Thread raffia strips or ribbon through the holes. Tie securely.

9. Carefully glue your pressed flowers and leaves onto the watercolor pages of the scrapbook. Underneath each flower and leaf write its name, along with any growing information you wish to remember about it. The onionskin paper will cover each page of flowers and protect it.

Flower Arranging

A ROSE BOUQUET

And the roses—the roses!

Roses are usually best displayed in crystal, silver, or porcelain containers. There are bowls especially designed for the old-fashioned types of roses with slender, flexible stems. These rose bowls are round with a narrow opening in the top so that the stems are held close together and the flowers are massed luxuriously.

A more modern way of holding roses in arrangements is to use a block of florist's foam, soaked in water and taped to the inside of the container or a wire "frog," a metal holder with fine spikes placed in the bottom of the container. With either device, the stems of the flowers can be stuck in and held in place.

To make a simple rose bouquet, you will need:

1 dozen roses, some in full bloom, some in the half-open stage

A rose bowl or other container

OPTIONAL:

A wire frog or a block of florist's foam

Floral tape

Ferns, ivy, or other greenery

1. If you are cutting the roses from your own rosebushes, cut them in the morning and put them immediately into a deep container filled with water. Keep the roses in a cool, dark place until you are ready to arrange them.

2. Take each rose from the water, trim off the lower leaves, and clip off the thorns. Hold the stem under water and cut off about an inch. (This keeps air bubbles from entering the stem and blocking the water channels.)

3. If you are using a rose bowl, just fill it with water and set it aside. If you are using a frog, place it in the middle of the container and tape it down with floral tape. If you are using florist's foam, cut it to fit the container, soak it thoroughly in water, and tape it into the container. Make sure there is plenty of water in the container you are using, then set it aside.

4. In one hand hold one of the half-opened roses as the central flower. With your other hand, arrange the other roses around the first rose in a circular pattern.

5. Hold the bouquet next to the container to decide where to cut the stems. The bottom row of roses should come just to the top rim of the container. Holding the stems of the bouquet under water, cut them so that the bottoms are even.

6. Place the bouquet into the container. If you are using a rose bowl or a container with a frog, you can put the entire bouquet in at once and adjust the individual blossoms as necessary. If you are using florist's foam, insert each stem into the foam individually, following the pattern of the arrangement you began with.

7. If desired, you can fill in any gaps with other greenery such as ivy or ferns.

A TOPIARY FLOWER
ARRANGEMENT

There were numbers of standard roses which had so spread their branches that they were like little trees.

Topiary, the art of shaping trees and shrubs, was featured in the gardens of Misselthwaite Manor. But you do not have to clip trees to enjoy topiary. You can arrange flowers to resemble topiary very easily.

To make a topiary flower arrangement, you will need:

1 4″ flowerpot
Styrofoam cut to fit the
*   flowerpot*
Floral foam ball, 4″ in diameter
*   (You may have to cut a*
*   block of floral foam into a*
*   rough ball shape if you*
*   cannot find it already*
*   formed.)*

24 slender twigs, 12–14″ long
3 rubber bands
2–3 dozen small flowers, such
*   as daisies, marigolds, or*
*   rosebuds*
6″ piece sheet moss or a
*   handful of Spanish moss*
Glue or pins
Raffia or ribbon

1. Set the flowerpot on a flat surface and press the Styrofoam firmly into it.

2. Soak the ball of floral foam in water so that it is thoroughly moistened.

3. Gather the twigs together into a bundle about one inch in diameter and secure them with rubber bands.

4. Stick one end of the bundle of sticks firmly into the Styrofoam so that it goes down to the bottom of the pot.

5. With a sharp stick or scissors, make a small hole in the floral foam ball about three quarters of an inch in diameter and a half-inch deep.

6. Set the ball of floral foam on top of the stick bundle so that the end of the bundle goes into the hole you have cut. Press the ball down so that it fits securely on top of the stick bundle.

7. Cut the flower stems to about two inches long.

8. With a toothpick or skewer, poke a hole into the floral foam ball at the very top. Insert a flower into the foam until the head of the flower rests on the foam.

9. Make another hole so that the petals of the next flower slightly overlap the petals of the first one, and insert another flower. Continue this process until the whole ball is densely covered with flowers.

10. Place moss on top of the Styrofoam in the pot to cover it completely. Secure it with a little glue or pins if necessary.

11. Tie a length of ribbon or raffia at the top of the stick bundle, next to the flower ball, and make a decorative bow. Carefully cut off any rubber bands that are still visible.

12. To keep the flower ball fresh, sprinkle or mist it with water several times a day.

A MINIATURE ARRANGEMENT

"Th' very little ones are snowdrops an' crocuses. . . ."

Mary's and Colin's breakfast trays and the tea trays brought to them in the afternoon would have had little flower arrangements on them. Look around your house for tiny objects that might make fun containers for miniature arrangements. A tiny doll-size teapot or cup, or even a small hollowed-out apple or other fruit would work beautifully.

To make a miniature arrangement, you will need:

A small container, such as a
   tiny teacup or a silver
   baby cup
3 or 4 small flowers

1 or 2 small fern leaves or ivy
   sprigs
Ribbon (optional)

1. Fill the small container about half full with water.

2. Arrange the flowers and leaves in your hand and cut off the stems to fit the container.

3. Place the arrangement in the container and adjust the flowers and leaves as necessary.

4. Tie a piece of ribbon around the stems of the flowers or around the container, if desired.

Skipping Activities

MARY'S SKIPPING ROPE

It was a strong, slender rope with a striped red and blue handle at each end, but Mary Lennox had never seen a skipping rope before.

Martha's mother, Mrs. Sowerby, bought Mary a skipping rope from a peddler. On fine days, Mary skipped outside on the walks in the manor gardens, but on rainy days she took her skipping rope to the large portrait galleries inside the manor and practiced her skips there.

To make a skipping rope similar to Mary's, you will need:

6–8' clothesline rope (available at hardware stores)
Scissors

½" paintbrush
2 ounces blue acrylic paint
2 ounces red acrylic paint

1. To determine the best length of rope for yourself, hold one end of the rope in each hand. Place one foot in the middle of the rope and step down on it firmly.

2. Raise the ends of the rope to your shoulders. Cut off any excess rope.

3. Tie a knot at each end of the rope.

4. To make "red and blue striped handles" for your skipping rope, paint a red stripe around the last two inches of each end of the rope as shown. Paint one of the knots at the end of the rope red.

5. When the red paint is dry, paint a two-inch blue stripe next to the red stripes as shown. Paint the knot at the other end of the rope blue.

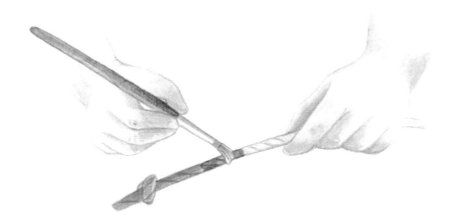

6. Finally, when the blue paint is dry, paint two inches of red next to the blue stripe.

Now you have a skipping rope with red and blue handles. Try it out with some of the following rhymes.

TRADITIONAL ENGLISH SKIPPING RHYMES

The skipping-rope was a wonderful thing. She counted and skipped, and skipped and counted, until her cheeks were quite red, and she was more interested than she had ever been since she was born.

At first Mary counted her skips but, like other girls her age, she could have chanted rhymes as she skipped, too.

Here are some traditional English skipping rhymes that Mary might have learned from Martha. The first one, of course, is the verse the English clergyman's children used to describe Mary.

1.

Mistress Mary, quite contrary,
How does your garden grow?
With silver bells and cockle shells
And pretty maids all in a row.

2.

Up the ladder and down the wall,
Penny an hour will serve us all.
You buy butter and I'll buy flour,
And we'll have a pudding in half an hour.
With salt, mustard, vinegar, pepper. . . .
(Repeat until you miss a step, then start over.)

3.

Bluebells, cockle shells,
Eavy, Ivy, Over!
This is how the alphabet goes,
A, B, C, D . . .

4.

Black currant, red currant, raspberry tart,
Tell me the name of my sweetheart,
A, B, C, D . . .
(When you miss a step, that letter is supposed
to tell you the first letter of your sweetheart's name.)

5.

Half a pound of tuppenny rice,
Half a pound of treacle.
Mix it up and make it nice,
Pop goes the weasel!

6.

Jelly on a plate,
Jelly on a plate,
Wibble, wobble, wibble, wobble,
Jelly on a plate.

Sausages in the pan,
Sausages in the pan,
Turn them over, turn them over,
Sausages in the pan.

Ghostie in the house,
Ghostie in the house,
Turn him out, turn him out,
Ghostie in the house.

7.

I am (your name), dressed in blue,
These are the actions I must do,
Salute to the captain, bow to the queen,
Twist right round and count fifteen.
1, 2, 3, 4 . . .
(Try to jump all the way to **15** without missing a step.)

For Birds in the Garden

ROBIN'S PICNIC TEA BASKET

The bird put his tiny head on one side and looked up at him with his soft bright eye which was like a black dewdrop. He seemed quite familiar and not the least afraid. He hopped about and pecked the earth briskly, looking for seeds and insects.

One quick way to attract robins is to dig and turn over a few shovelfuls of earth. You will soon see a robin hopping close by to see if it can snatch an earthworm or two from the soil. Ben Weatherstaff was digging in the kitchen garden when Mary first met him, and the robin soon joined them and hopped onto Ben's spade.

Robins also like seeds and suet (beef fat you can buy from the butcher). You can prepare a special teatime treat for the robins and other birds in your neighborhood to enjoy.

To make a picnic tea basket for the birds, you will need:

*1 small basket with a handle
   (a "half-round" basket
   works well)
¼ cup vegetable oil (optional)
6–8 fresh green leaves*

*¼ cup oatmeal
2 tablespoons chopped peanuts
¼ cup dry breadcrumbs
½ cup mixed birdseed
½ cup suet, finely chopped*

1. If the basket is untreated with varnish or paint, brush it inside and out with vegetable oil. This will help preserve it.

2. Line the basket with fresh green leaves. Set aside.

3. Mix the oatmeal, peanuts, breadcrumbs, and birdseed in a large bowl. Add the chopped suet. Mix thoroughly.

4. With your hands, roll the mixture into balls about one inch in diameter; flatten them slightly to look like little tea cakes.

5. Place the suet cakes in the basket.

6. Hang the basket of suet cakes on the branch of a tree.

7. Replace the green leaves and replenish the suet cakes as needed.

BIRD BATH

There, indeed, was the robin, and she thought he looked nicer than ever. His red waistcoat was as glossy as satin and he flirted his wings and tail and tilted his head and hopped about with all sorts of lively graces.

Birds love to splash in shallow puddles and bird baths, especially when they are interested in finding a mate. Provide a spot in your garden for a bird bath and watch the birds preen!

To make a simple bird bath, you will need:

15 4"-thick bricks or flat stones
1 18" terra-cotta plant saucer or other wide, shallow pot

1. Place three bricks (or flat stones) so they form a triangle on a flat, sunny spot, perhaps in the middle of a flower bed.

2. Stack more bricks on top of the first three as shown until you have a pedestal one and a half to two feet high.

3. Place the saucer on top of the pedestal. Pour water into the saucer.

4. Replenish the water as needed.

NEST-BUILDING STATION

"Eh! the nests as'll be here come springtime," he said. "It'd be th' safest nestin' place in England. No one never comin' near an' tangles o' trees an' roses to build in. I wonder all th' birds on th' moor don't build here."

Every kind of bird builds its own style of nest and uses a variety of materials for building. Crows and rooks, like Dickon's Soot, make their nests of twigs, grass, and mud. Missel thrushes, the bird Dickon sketched on the note he left for Mary that said "I will cum back," build their nests of dirt and small plants.

Robins like to nest in dense shrubbery. First they make a little cushion of dead leaves in the branches of a tree or bush. Then they construct a small nest of moss and leaves. They line the nest with hair to make it very soft for the female bird to incubate the eggs and to protect the newly hatched baby birds.

You can gather together raw materials for a nest for the birds in your garden.

To make a nest-building station for birds, you will need:

1 square foot chicken wire with 1″ holes
2 cups leaves, green or dry
1 bag Spanish moss (available at craft stores)

18″ 20-gauge wire (or picture-hanging wire)

1. Wearing gardening gloves, loosely bend the chicken wire into a ball about the size of a grapefruit, leaving a small opening at the top (see illustration).

2. Stuff the leaves loosely into the ball of wire; press the opening of the wire ball closed.

3. Separate bits of moss and stuff them into the holes of the chicken wire.

4. Thread the wire through one of the holes and make a loop. Twist the ends together to hold the loop closed. Hang the nest building station on a tree branch. Add the following items to the station as you find them, poking them into the moss as you wish:

Pieces of string or thread   *Cobwebs*
Pieces of pinecones   *Seedpods*
Small twigs and sticks   *Grass clippings*
Acorns   *Shreds of paper*
Feathers

Conclusion

The Secret Garden is more than a simple story about children finding a forgotten garden behind walls. It is also about the miracle of growth and renewal. The garden itself was a miracle, in that it kept growing and blooming although it had not been carefully tended for years. Mary Lennox and Colin Craven experienced miracles of their own in the secret garden, both discovering that they were stronger and more resilient than anyone had ever encouraged them to believe. Archibald Craven experienced the miracle of a renewed interest in life and the joys of being a real father to Colin.

The secret garden could not share its special beauty until the door in its high, locked walls was opened to those who could nurture and appreciate the beauty within. The same was true for Mary, Colin, and Mr. Craven. All three had allowed walls of grief and disappointment to block happiness from their hearts. Even the gardener, Ben Weatherstaff, had let the walls of loneliness and cynicism build up around him. Happiness came to each of them through the magic that seemed to rise from the secret garden, and they took that happiness with them from inside the garden's walls into the world beyond.

The Secret Garden reminds us that whether we are rich or poor, privileged or neglected, nurture and careful cultivation will make the difference between a satisfying life and one that is stunted and forever struggling for air and light.

Language of The Secret Garden

The station-master spoke to Mrs. Medlock in a rough, good-natured way, pronouncing his words in a queer broad fashion which Mary found out afterward was Yorkshire.

*T*he Secret Garden is filled with many unfamiliar words. Mary had lived in several worlds by the time she was ten years old, and each world had its own unique culture and language. She grew up in northern India, where her father was stationed as a British officer (at that time, India was a part of the British Empire). Though she lived in India, she spoke English and learned English customs, but she learned some Indian words and customs, too.

In nineteenth-century England, the class structure was layered and quite rigid. Each class spoke English, but classes had distinct accents and used different terms for describing things. Mary spoke with a middle-to-upper-class English accent, but when she found herself living in Yorkshire in the north of England, near the Scottish border, she determined to learn "a bit o' Yorkshire" so that she could speak more naturally with Martha, Dickon, Ben Weatherstaff, and Mrs. Sowerby.

For those who are not familiar with the Indian, Yorkshire, and English terms sprinkled throughout *The Secret Garden*, here is a glossary of some of the words along with the way they were used in the book and their meanings.

Indian

ayah native Indian nursemaid ("'My Ayah dressed me, of course.'" —Ch. 1)

fakir beggar; Hindu person who rejects personal comforts for religious reasons; snake charmer ("Because she was born in India where there were fakirs." —Ch. 23)

Hindustani One of the languages of northern India ("began to stroke and pat his hand and sing a very low little chanting song in Hindustani." —Ch. 13)

Mem Sahib (or Missie Sahib) Indian term of respect similar to madam ("when Mary was born, she handed her over to the care of an Ayah . . . who was made to understand that if she wished to please the Mem Sahib, she was to keep the child out of sight as much as possible." —Ch. 1)

mahout person who leads an elephant; elephant's caretaker ("in a cabinet were about a hundred little elephants made of ivory. They were of different sizes, and some had their mahouts or palanquins on their backs." —Ch. 6)

palanquins (see "mahouts") enclosed compartment for passengers riding on an elephant

Rajah Indian prince ("'Once in India I saw a boy who was a Rajah.'" —Ch. 14)

salaam a low bow made with one or both hands touching the forehead ("They made salaams and called them 'protector of the poor' and names of that sort." —Ch. 4)

Yorkshire

bachelder bachelor (unmarried adult male) ("'If I wasn't a bachelder, an' tha' was a wench o' mine,' he cried, 'I'd give thee a hidin'.'" —Ch. 21)

besom ("bee-zum") rough broom made of twigs tied around a heavy stick for a handle ("'A scrawny, buttermilk-faced young besom, allus askin' questions.'" —Ch. 21)

clemmin' thirst ("'and found th' little 'un half dead wi' cold an' clemmin'" —Ch. 19)

forrad ("fahrd") forward; bold ("'Has tha' begun tha' courtin' this early in th' season? Tha'rt too forrad.'" —Ch. 4)

graidely ("grye-dly") excellent ("'He's took a graidely fancy to thee.'" —Ch. 18)

marred spoiled; moody ("'A more marred-looking one I never saw in my life,' Mrs. Medlock thought." —Ch. 2)

missel thrush the largest of the thrush family of birds; it feeds on fruit and insects and especially likes mistletoe and holly berries; it also enjoys apples, bread, and table scraps ("'That there's a picture of a missel thrush on her nest.'" —Ch. 13)

moithered ("mye-thered") flustered (fair moithered: completely flustered) ("'Mother's a good-tempered women but she gets fair moithered.'" —Ch. 6)

nesh delicate ("'I wasn't brought up nesh enough.'" —Ch. 11)

pluck spirit ("'Tha's got too much pluck in thee.'" —Ch. 22)

rose cold spring allergy thought to be caused by rose pollen ("'He'd

been readin' in a paper about people gettin' somethin' he called "rose cold" an' he began to sneeze an' said he'd got it.'" —Ch. 14)

tha' you (thee) ("'Tha's got a bit o' garden, hasn't tha'?'" —Ch. 10)

victuals food ("'Run on an' get thy victuals.'" —Ch. 11)

wench country girl or young woman ("'Art tha' th' little wench from India?'" he asked. —Ch. 4)

wick alive ("'It's as wick or you or me.'" —Ch. 11)

wutherin' the deep, mysterious whistling sound the wind makes blowing through trees, around windows ("'Listen to th' wind wutherin' round the house.'" —Ch. 5)

English

blacking brush brush used to apply blacking (a lead compound) to an iron grate or cookstove ("Martha sat up on her heels, with her blacking brush in her hand, and laughed, without seeming the least out of temper." —Ch. 4)

bread sauce gravy thickened with bread crumbs ("'Not a mouthful of that lovely young fowl and bread sauce did they set a fork into yesterday.'" —Ch 24)

brougham enclosed carriage with four wheels; the driver's box is curved underneath to allow the smaller front wheels to turn ("A brougham stood on the road before the little outside platform." —Ch. 3)

cinders bits of charred wood or coal ("a young housemaid . . . was kneeling on the hearth-rug raking out the cinders noisily." —Ch. 4)

crêpe thin cloth, usually silk or wool, with a pebbly texture; black crêpe was worn in Victorian England as a sign of mourning ("her limp light hair straggled from under her black crêpe hat." —Ch. 2)

hobnailed boot work boot with a heavy sole nailed on with pegs or nails that have large, thick heads ("He stood up and rested one

hobnailed boot on top of his spade while he looked her over." —Ch. 10)

mantle a loosely fitting cloak ("She wore a very purple dress, a black silk mantle with jet fringe on it." —Ch. 2)

moor high, rolling terrain in parts of Yorkshire that supports few trees; "white moors" are covered with coarse grass; "black moors" contain heath and peat, used as fuel. ("'It isn't fields nor mountains, it's just miles and miles and miles of wild land that nothing grows on but heather and gorse and broom, and nothing lives on but wild ponies and sheep.'" —Ch. 3)

rockery rock garden ("'Why don't you put a heap of stones there and pretend it is a rockery?'" —Ch. 2)

ruff pleated collar popular in the sixteenth and seventeenth centuries ("Some were pictures of children . . . with big ruffs around their necks. —Ch. 6)

salver serving tray ("The man held a salver with some letters on it." —Ch. 27)

scullery-maid female kitchen servant assigned to wash dishes, scrub pots and pans, and other menial chores ("'An' if it wasn't, it was little Betty Butterworth, th' scullery-maid.'" —Ch. 5)

shilling British coin equaling 1/20 of a British pound or 12 pennies or pence (sixteen shillings would total 192 pence, about $4 at that time) ("'There's twelve of us an' my father only gets sixteen shilling a week.'" —Ch. 4)

sovereign British gold coin, worth a pound, or twenty shillings ("He smiled at their friendly grins and took a golden sovereign from his pocket." —Ch. 27)

tuppence two pence (pennies) ("'I'm just goin' to take tuppence out of it to buy that child a skippin'-rope.'" —Ch. 8)

vicarage residence of the parish priest (Anglican) ("Then they had passed a church and a vicarage." —Ch. 3)

wardrobe large cupboard for storing clothing; commonly used before closets began to be built into bedrooms ("the clothes Martha took

124

from the wardrobe were not the ones she had worn when she arrived the night before with Mrs. Medlock." —Ch. 4)

waterproof long raincoat or other raingear oiled or waxed so that water will not penetrate the cloth ("The rain seemed to be streaming down more heavily than ever and everybody in the station wore wet and glistening waterproofs." —Ch. 3)

white-thorn knobstick stick with a round knob or ball on the end, made from a branch of a hawthorn tree ("'I'm as tough as a white-thorn knobstick.'" —Ch. 11)

Bibliograpy

*H*ere are some of the many resources consulted in writing *Inside the Secret Garden*.

Beeton, Mrs. Isabella. *The Book of Household Management*. London: S. O. Beeton, 1861.

Burnett, Frances Hodgson. *In the Garden*. Boston: The Medici Society of America, 1925.

———. *My Robin*. New York: Frederick A. Stokes Company, 1912.

———. *The One I Knew Best of All*. New York: Charles Scribner's Sons, 1983.

———. *The Secret Garden*. New York: HarperCollins, 1990.

Burnett, Vivian. *The Romantick Lady: The Life Story of an Imagination*. New York: Charles Scribner's Sons, 1927.

Burton, Robert. *Pocket Bird Feeder Handbook: A Guide to Attracting and Observing Garden Birds*. London: Dorling Kindersley, 1990.

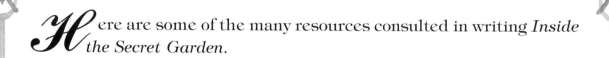

Campbell, Susan. *Walled Kitchen Gardens*. Princes Risborough, Buckinghamshire, UK: Shire Publications, 1998.

Cooper, Nicholas. *English Manor Houses*. London: Weidenfeld & Nicholson Ltd., 1990.

Corey, Melinda, and George Ochoa, eds. *The Encyclopedia of the Victorian World: A Reader's Companion to the People, Places, Events, and Everyday Life of the Victorian Era*. New York: Henry Holt and Company, 1996.

Cruse, Eléonore. *Roses: Old Roses and Species Roses*. Cologne, Germany: Evergreen, 1998.

Dickerson, Brent C. *The Old Rose Advisor*. Portland, Oregon: Timber Press, Inc., 1992.

Dierauff, Eva, and Anny Jacob. *Old Garden Roses and Selected Modern Hybrids*. New York: Thames and Hudson Ltd., 1988.

Great Maytham Hall. London: Country Houses Association.

Kellett, Arnold. *Dictionary of Yorkshire Dialect, Tradition and Folklore*. Otley, West Yorkshire: Smith Settle Ltd., 1994.

Modern Practical Cookery. London: Amalgamated Press, Ltd., c. 1930.

Persey, Amanda. *Favourite Yorkshire Recipes*. Sevenoaks, England: J. Salmon Ltd., no date.

Reilly, Ann. *The Rose*. New York: Portland House, 1989.

Talbot, Rob, and Robin Whiteman. *The Yorkshire Moors & Dales*. London: Weidenfeld & Nicholson Ltd., 1991.

Thwaite, Ann. *Waiting for the Party: The Life of Frances Hodgson Burnett*. Boston: David R. Godine, 1991.

Turner, Ernest Sackville. *What the Butler Saw: Two Hundred and Fifty Years of the Servant Problem*. New York: St. Martin's Press, 1963.

Index